for every Student's Success

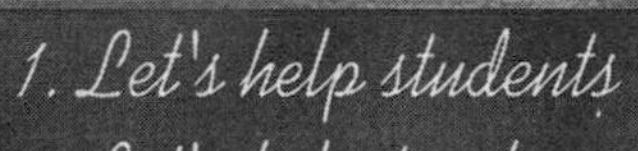

Robert A. Rohm Ph.D.

A Special Teachers Section by Pete Hinojosa

To learn more about personality styles
and to get four free online lessons,
please go to:
www.personalityinsights.com
On the home page click on the free
offer icon that says:
"Take the 4-part online course for
better relationships."
We hope you enjoy the lessons!

A+ Ideas for Every Student's Success

Robert A. Rohm Ph. D.

A Special Teachers Section by Pete Hinojosa

P.O. Box 28592 Atlanta, GA 30358-0592

www.personalityinsights.com

Editor – Beth McLendon
Cover Design, Layout and Graphics – Pedro A. Gonzalez

Published by
Personality Insights, Inc.
P.O. Box 28592
Atlanta, GA 30358-0592
1.800.509.DISC

www.personalityinsights.com

ISBN 0-9641080-9-7

Second Edition, September 2006

Printed in the United States of America

Table of Contents

Table of Contents continued...

Dedication

When I first went into the field of education, I thought my life would be primarily focused on teaching students academic information. Boy was I wrong! As a former school administrator, I quickly learned that there were three groups of people that I had to deal with each day: students, teachers and parents. That combination seemed like an intertwined threefold cord. They all connected with each other, and whichever way one group pulled, the other two seemed to follow!

I soon learned that teaching is not simply about dispensing information to a classroom full of students. It is about learning to work with different types of students, their parents (or guardians) and other teachers. A Carnegie Foundation study has shown that technical skills, beginning with intelligence and developed through education and experience, accounts for only 15% of success in the workplace. The other 85% of workplace success comes from people skills! These skills are developed through learning better ways to behave and interact. The reason for this book is to help all three groups (students, teachers and parents) learn how to build people skills in order to help them succeed.

To Students: As I write these words, I am 54 years old. I have graduated from 5 different colleges and universities in my lifetime. I have been a child, a teenager and an adult. I have walked in your shoes. If I could go back and be your age again and be back in school and if I could only take one "set of information" with me - the information in this book is what I would want to know. It has taken me a lifetime to acquire it. Now, it is available for you to learn in only a few hours. Learning it is fairly easy. Putting it into practice will take some time, but you can do it. It is a lot like riding a bicycle; you fall off a few times, but you will get the hang of it pretty quickly. Then, you can use it for the rest of your life.

Do not try to "fix" your teachers or your parents. Focus on "fixing" yourself. Your teachers and parents are not perfect people. Neither are you. Neither am I. However, we are down the road a little farther than you, and we want the best for you. It may not seem that way now, but in time you will "see it" more clearly. Trust me, we have your best interest in mind. We are not better than you or smarter than you, but we are more experienced than you. If you learn to use good "people skills," your life will be much more enjoyable.

To Teachers: First, the stories you are about to read will entertain you. Each story is a real classroom scenario shared by teachers from kindergarten through senior high school. After learning about the DISC system of personality behavior traits through a summer training program, teachers were assigned to write their best case studies from their own classroom experiences applying the principles of DISC. Some of these stories will make you laugh, some will make you cry and, hopefully, all will make you think.

Secondly, these stories will provide you with a better understanding of the DISC Model of Human Behavior and how it works, specifically in the classroom environment. Through reading each story, you will learn the dynamics of DISC information and why knowing and using DISC on a daily basis is important.

Finally, you will take from each story a practical application of DISC information. You will obtain ideas, review specific suggestions, and learn how DISC principles can work for you, as well as how to make it a reality in your classroom or at home.

Let there be no doubt that one of the most important dynamics that you, as a teacher, bring into your classroom environment is your own personality style, along with your own personal teaching style. After all, part of the motivation that drew you into the teaching profession was the fact that you see things in a unique way and want to share that information and knowledge with others. However, this next thought is the key: because teachers are the mature adults in the classroom environment, they must be the ones to learn how to adapt and adjust the information which they present to their class in order to raise the students to new heights of learning. Unless a teacher has high expectations for his students and communicates information in a way that is helpful to individual personality types, the students will not achieve an excellent educational experience. The teacher will end up dispensing information in the one way that seems best to him. That may or may not be helpful to a student. If, on the other hand, the teacher is aware that different personality styles really do exist in the classroom and specifically teaches to each type, then the educational experience will flourish.

Someone wisely noted, "The teacher has not taught anything until the student has learned." This puts the responsibility squarely upon the teacher's shoulders for communicating information to students clearly and concisely. As an educator, this makes me very uncomfortable, but, nevertheless, I believe it to be true. If I am going to reach my students, I must find a way in which to reach them.

Zig Ziglar says, "People are already motivated... to do exactly what they want to do! My job is to help 'create a climate' or 'engineer an environment' to help each person want to do better in his daily life." By understanding personality styles and what best motivates each type, you can become an excellent "climate creator" to help each person that you work with to be better motivated to achieve extraordinary results!

Teachers already understand the fact that their students are going to be different. This, however, is only one step in being a good teacher. A good teacher knows specifically how students are individually different and what motivates them. You have heard the old saying, "You can lead a horse to water, but you can't make him drink." That is true; however, there is another part of that saying that is equally true, "But, you can salt his oats and make him thirsty." It is our job as teachers (and parents) to learn how to better "salt their oats."

Research seems to indicate that students learn a great deal by their personalities and related learning styles. The teacher must carefully take into consideration exactly what can be done to work with those differences, rather than working against them. Unless the teacher is aware of all of these factors, he will fall into the trap of trying to teach every student the same way and expect the same results. Ironically, we, as teachers, are the first ones to recognize that all of our students do not have the same needs, desires, strengths or weaknesses. Yet, we continue to try to teach them all the same way. Why? Probably because the way we teach is the way that seems or feels best to us. Our teaching methodology is often the way that seemed to work best in helping us to learn in our own educational experience. The information contained in this book will hopefully enlighten teachers and parents to do a better job in connecting to their students and children in a new and more successful way.

To Parents: As a father of four children of my own (and several other "adopted" children), I know what it means to have the heart of a parent. I love my children. You love your children. There is nothing that you would not do to help them have a good life. I have seen parents take on unbelievable additional sacrifices in order to help their children be able to experience and have things that they otherwise would not be able to have. Sometimes it takes years and years before children grow up and realize how hard their parents had to work in order for them to have a better life. Gratitude comes slowly. . . but it eventually arrives!

Perhaps nothing is more important than parents helping their children receive a good education. After all, most children spend 13 years in K5 - 12th grade. (8 hours a day x 5 days a week x 36 school weeks a year x 13 years = 18,720 hours!) It is during these hours that our children acquire most of the educational tools that they will use the rest of their lives. (This includes reading, writing, math, spelling, grammar, typing and computer skills.) Investing that much time makes the matter of one's education a matter of vital importance. A child's education guides him and influences nearly every decision that he makes every day of his life.

Every parent knows that there are many differences in their children. We cannot "raise them" all the same way. What motivates one child may do just the opposite for another. If ever there was a group of people who know there is a difference in personality types, it is parents. The section in this book for parents may be the most important information (as well as the greatest gift) that you could ever have in order to help your children reach their fullest potential.

Whether you are a student, teacher or parent, these real stories are designed to give you helpful tips and practical applications that you can use on a daily basis. Each section is broken down by grade level: Lower Elementary, Upper Elementary, Middle School and High School. We have tried to select the very best examples in order to give the reader a clear and vivid picture as to the importance of seeing how valuable and powerful the DISC system is when used on a daily basis. Also, we show specific challenges which each personality style brings to the classroom, along with practical solutions and suggestions to help make the learning experience more successful.

As you read this book, it is my hope that you will silently think to yourself, "This is really powerful information. I only wish I had known it sooner!" If you think that way, you will be eager to put this knowledge into practice. That is where the payoff really occurs. I know that it is your desire to do better in the field of education. So, with over thirty years of educational experience, I offer to you, the reader, some of the wisest insights I could give you to make your journey easier, more fun, and a lot more successful. There is something for everyone in this book. Share it with your students, teachers and parents. It will help everyone start "singing off the same page!"

Foreword

I first met Robert Rohm in 1975 when he was a young school principal. I could tell that he loved what he did. After all, spending time with children was the perfect thing for him to do everyday, since he was simply a grown child himself!

Education was his passion. So as we had lunch together, he asked me question after question about how to help students get the most out of their educational experience. I knew then that his students and his faculty would be hungry to learn, because he was hungry to learn. You always produce after your own kind, and he was setting the "learning example" by having an insatiable appetite for learning.

Over the years, our paths have crossed several times. Robert attended several events where I was speaking. He always had a notebook in his hands to make a few notes of what I said and pages of what he thought. He was always listening, learning and thinking, and he wanted to help others to be learning and thinking with him as well.

In 1991, he started his public speaking career. It took off, not simply because he was a gifted speaker, but because he had real content in his presentation. His material was taken from his own personal life experiences, as well as information that he had learned in the 5 colleges from which he graduated. A powerful message, a gifted speaker, a well-educated person and a lot of enthusiasm and humor make an unbeatable combination!

One weekend, Robert Rohm, Zig Ziglar and I were the three guest speakers at a business convention in Washington

D.C. Zig spoke first, Robert spoke second and then I spoke last. Zig and I both have over 50 years of speaking experience, and we EACH have more than 40 years more experience than he does! Yet, I can tell you this, his information was the highlight of the convention. Much of that information is in this book. I only wish my wife, Gloria, and I had known these truths when we were raising our six children.

So, feel blessed as you read and learn... because you are!!

Charlie "*Tremendous*" Jones
Executive Books, Inc.
Mechanicsburg, PA

Acknowledgments

I want to publicly thank a few people for all the hard work that they put into this project, so that this book would become a reality.

First, I want to thank my editor, proofreader, spell checker and correct tense coordinator, eagle-eye Beth McLendon. Her labor alone has made this book easier to read and understand. As a teacher herself, her goal was to help create a work that would make the teaching profession more enjoyable for all teachers, parents and students. In my opinion, she successfully "over-reached" her goal! Thanks, Beth!

I want to thank Pete Hinojosa. His daily "on the job" experience has made the truths found in this book come alive. This information is not some theory discussed somewhere in an ivory tower. He has helped to make this information practical, applicable, duplicatable, transferable and most of all useable. Pete works full time in Houston, Texas, in the public school system. He helps students, teachers and parents get more value out of their educational experience. Thanks, Pete.

I want to thank Lisa Bearse. She helped in the developmental stage of the classroom stories. As a teacher, she has mastered the ability to use DISC information in the classroom in order to help her students. If ever there was someone who knew how to work *with* her students, rather than working *against* them, it is Lisa. Thanks, Lisa!

I want to thank my Administrative Director, Deborah Mullen, for typing and coordinating all of the material between the shared-files in our office computers. Someone has to know where all the information is at all times and which story goes where. Losing precious information on work already completed can be a nightmare. Somehow she kept everything together until the very end of the project. Deborah is a fantastic Administrative Director! Thanks, Deborah!

I want to thank our Graphic Artist at Personality Insights, Inc., Pedro A. Gonzalez. He is a master of his trade! I can meet with Pedro and tell him a picture that I see in my head. He then goes to his office and in two or three hours, he produces the very image that I saw earlier in my mind... only a little better! He amazes me. Thanks, Pedro.

Finally, I want to thank all the teachers that I sat under as a student, and I want to thank my fellow colleagues that worked with me when I was a school administrator. All these teachers were the ones who actually gave me the idea for this book. I only wish I had better understood this material when I was in those educational environments. I could have been a much better student during my "learning days" and a much better principal during my "leadership days." Anyway, to all of you, wherever you are, living or not, thank you ... and may God bless you for all you mean to me to this very day!

Before You Start

Brief Review of DISC

It should be stated, at the beginning of this book, that we are basing this book on the **DISC** Model of Human Behavior. Over the years, we have introduced this material to thousands of parents, teachers and business owners in order to increase their effectiveness in their own chosen professions.

The following simple introduction to **DISC** is necessary, before you will be ready to gain insights from this book.

GET THE PICTURE

Most people have predictable patterns of behavior and specific personality types. There are four basic personality types, also known as temperaments. The four types are like four parts of a pie. Before looking at each of the four parts, let's look at the pie in two parts. These two parts are designated as **outgoing** and **reserved.** Think of it this way: some people are more outgoing, while others are more reserved.

Outgoing people are more active and optimistic. **Reserved** types are more passive and careful. One type is not better than the other. Both types of behavior are needed, and both are important. Outgoing types need to learn how to be more steady and cautious. Reserved types need to learn how to be more dominant and inspiring.

There is another way to divide the pie. It can be divided into **task-oriented** and **people-oriented.** Some people are more task-oriented, and some are more relationship-oriented. **Task-oriented** types need to learn to relate better to others and become more interactive and sharing. **People-oriented** individuals need to learn to be more focused on doing tasks or things. They need to be more directing and correcting.

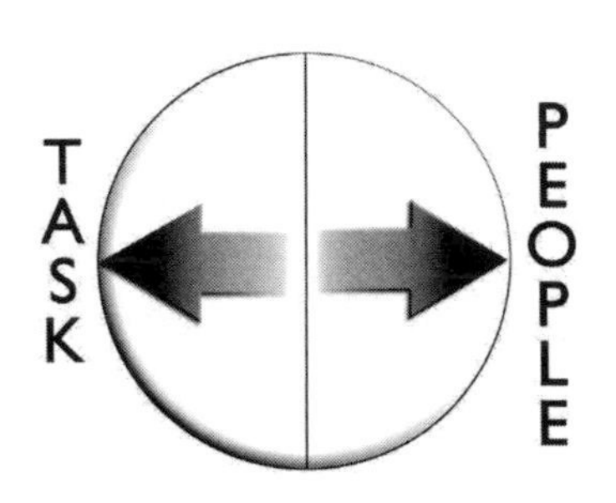

Now, we can have a pie divided into four parts. We can visualize the four parts: D, I, S and C. Those people who we say are predominately "***D***" types are outgoing and task-oriented. Those who we say are predominately "***I***" types are outgoing and people-oriented. Those who we say are predominately "***S***" types are reserved and people-oriented. Those who we say are predominately "***C***" types are reserved and task-oriented.

The "***D***" type can be described with words like: Dominant, Direct, Demanding, Decisive, Determined and Doer.

The "***I***" type can be described with words like: Inspiring, Influencing, Inducing, Interactive, Impressive and Interested in people.

The "***S***" type can be described with words like: Supportive, Steady, Stable, Sweet, Sensitive and Status Quo.

The "***C***" type can be described with words like: Cautious, Calculating, Competent, Consistent, Contemplative and Careful.

D = Dominant
I = Inspiring
S = Supportive
C = Cautious

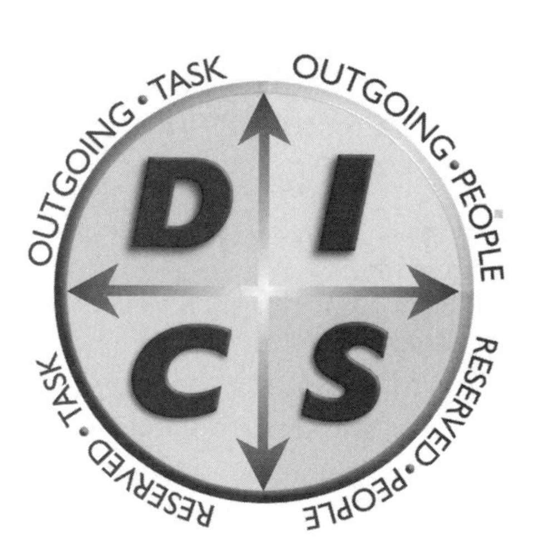

No one is purely a "***D***" or an "***I***" or an "***S***" or a "***C***". Everyone is a unique blend of these four types. If someone says that he is an "***I / D***" personality blend, that means that he is highest in the traits of the "***I***" (Inspiring type), and that he is next highest in the traits of the "***D***" (Dominant type). This, of course, is true of the other traits, as well.

Suggestions to help make this book Fun, Practical and Applicable!

The stories in this book are designed to create awareness and understanding of the value of using ***DISC*** personality information in the classroom. Individual teachers will be given information and encouragement to begin the process of learning the basics of personality information and then help in using that information to improve a classroom setting. The stories you will read in this book make great case studies for your classroom students or your family dinner table discussion. Each story demonstrates an understanding of how different personality styles think, feel and act. We all approach situations in a different manner. The question for you to ask yourself should be, "Am I able to evaluate a situation in an objective manner by understanding personality styles and come to a balanced conclusion for everyone concerned?" When you are able to do that, you will be able to interact with other people in a new, improved way.

Here are a few suggested questions to use with the stories:

1. How do you think the teacher was feeling as the situation unfolded? Why?
2. What did you learn about the "***D***" type from this story?
3. What did you learn about the "***I***" type from this story?
4. What did you learn about the "***S***" type from this story?
5. What did you learn about the "***C***" type from this story?
6. What could have been done differently by someone in the story to make his situation turn out better?
7. What behavior traits did you learn from individuals in the story that will help you to be wiser in making future decisions?

Life is a wonderful teacher. Most of us will be confronted with the lessons that we need to know whether we want to or not. The wiser the choices that we make, the better off we will be. Hopefully, the stories in this book will give you new insight to help you become wiser and more successful in all that you do. ***God bless you!***

Introduction

As you read the following information, please keep in mind that we are not trying to "stereotype" anyone. We would be the first to promote the fact that personality types can and do cross all kinds of differences (male/female, birth order, age differences, race, religion, nationality, etc.). However, in order to more clearly paint a picture of how each style acts, interacts and reacts with each other, we have chosen to use stories and illustrations to more effectively communicate our point. It is not our intent to label, categorize, analyze, pigeonhole or put anyone in a box. It is our intent, however, to better understand people...ourselves as well as others.

We would also like to point out that because of the redundancy in reading both pronouns: he/she or him/her, we have chosen to use the simpler, more traditional method of the masculine gender. However, no one should think that I am a male chauvinist. I once lived with four daughters. I was a minority in a sorority. My biggest fear in life was going to the bathroom at night and dying of pantyhose strangulation! I did survive that season of my life. Having said that, let us now get started!

One of the biggest weaknesses in our school system is a lack of understanding regarding basic differences in personality styles.

Consider the following scenario:

A high "**C**" teacher enters the classroom well prepared with lesson plans in hand. She wants to enlighten the minds of her students. She believes that her purpose is to teach the academic subject to which she has been assigned. She is educated and academically equipped to accomplish the task at hand.

A high "***I***" student enters the classroom. He has a lot on his mind, the least of which is academic information. He has not come to learn. He has come to see his friends and meet new ones! This boy is ready to have fun, and he has a comment to make related to just about everything. He loves people; therefore, school is simply an environment for socializing. The only reason he is taking the course is because he needs the credit to graduate.

The father is a high "***D***". He wants results. He knows life is challenging, so a good education simply becomes a means to an end. He expects the teacher to teach and the student to learn. What is so complicated about that? He wants and expects good grades, few problems and little distractions from his busy schedule. If the teacher cannot handle her classroom, she needs to be replaced. If his son will not behave, he needs to be punished. It is just that simple.

The mother is a high "***S***". She spends a lot of time feeling distressed about the challenges the teacher must face each day. She is concerned, because she does not know, down deep inside, whether or not her child is receiving a good education. But, she does not want to say anything to anybody, because it might upset someone. So, she tries her best to simply be a referee and keep the peace as much as possible between all parties concerned. She keeps her bottle of Mylanta close by her.

Now let's take these four people and imagine that all four have suddenly received a working knowledge of personality style information. In other words, all four now understand the ***DISC*** information, and they are applying it to their daily situations. Consider the significant difference that the ***DISC*** information can make:

The teacher recognizes that she is a high "***C***". She knows that she is ready to teach, and she has high expectations for her students. More importantly, she knows that her job assignment is not simply to teach academic information. Her job is to teach students! (And, there is quite a big difference in those two ideas.) When she prepares her lesson plans, she includes some variety in her teaching methods in order to meet the needs of each of the four personality types. (Those will be explained in this book.) She realizes that her students do not know much about personality styles, so she becomes the one to adapt and work differently with each student in order to motivate each one to do his best work. She believes that a large part of the success of each student depends upon her own ability to help inspire each child to do his best work. *That is why she is called the teacher!*

The high "***I***" child enters the classroom recognizing the fact that his personality could be his worst enemy. The classroom is not a place primarily for his fun and games – not to mention all his "cutesy" comments about everything imaginable. He tries to get a seat close to the front, so he can listen better as well as stay focused longer. He does not want to sit beside any of his friends who could easily distract him or get him into trouble. He listens, takes notes, asks questions, acts interested and keeps his mouth under control. He realizes that even though the class may not be a lot of fun right now, the information will be beneficial to him in his life, and it will create future opportunities for him later. He understands that life isn't always fun and games. As Yogi Berra once said, "Hard work ain't easy!"

The high "**D**" father still wants results; however, he is also aware that people have feelings, and relationships are involved in this process. He is willing to take the approach of a "coach" rather than a "dictator." He feels it is important to keep the proper lines of communication open between all parties involved, and he further realizes that it will not happen if everyone is living in fear or walking around on eggshells. He shares with the teacher and his son any view or suggestion that he has. Also, he sincerely listens to the teacher and his son. He accepts any suggestions that the teacher or student has for him as well. He creates a teamwork environment and a "win-win" situation for all concerned.

The high "**S**" mom thinks that she has died and gone to heaven! There is peace and harmony at home as well as in the classroom. She does not live in a state of uncertainty as to when the next unexpected conflict may occur. She knows everyone is working together and pulling in the same direction. She becomes a helpful resource to everyone concerned. The teacher appreciates her "class mom" spirit. Her son has someone to help him on difficult or challenging assignments. Her husband appreciates her helpfulness, and together they create some good times and lasting memories together.

Does the second scenario sound too good to be true? Well... it is possible. When everyone starts working together, "singing off the same page," real harmony and teamwork can occur. Where there is genuine understanding and a willingness to grow together, there can be results beyond your wildest dreams. And doesn't that sound like a life worthy of the attempt to experience?

Symbol Explanation

Classroom Scenario

This icon appears before each case study. It represents the actual classroom scenario as told from the teacher's point of view. This is the ***What***. (As in, *what's going on!*)

Bits & Pieces

This icon appears before each section that explains ***How DISC*** works. It cites examples from the actual classroom scenario and goes into detail about ***How DISC*** works.

Knowing Why

This icon appears before each section that explains ***Why*** knowing ***DISC*** is important. It explains the insights and the helpful information that a teacher can obtain about students through an understanding of the principles found in using the ***DISC*** Model of Human Behavior.

Great Ideas

This icon appears before each section that explains ***How*** to ***Apply DISC*** in a practical and easy way in the classroom. This section gives suggestions on ***How*** to use the knowledge obtained from ***DISC*** to improve lesson plans and classroom management.

Go Fly A Kite

Occasionally, in March, I take my kindergarten class outdoors to fly kites. What happens during these outings helps me remember why this activity is something which I am only willing to do occasionally, rather than every March!

Each child brings a kite that we use as a classroom decoration until the perfect windy day arrives. Jacob, my High "***D***" student, insists his kite is the biggest and the best. Jesse, my High "***I***" student, thinks her pink Barbie kite is breathtakingly beautiful! Brittany, my High "***S***" student, quietly carries her kite and ducks her head as she walks around the room. She is being careful not to knock down any of the hanging kites. Casey, my High "**C**" student, wants to know if Scotch tape will mess up her kite and why I did not hang her kite in the classroom window.

We are all exited that today is the day to fly our kites. After going over the rules, we all head to the playground. Jacob runs ahead of us and scurries down the hill. He doesn't let go of the kite string, and, of course, it won't fly. He immediately displays his disappointment with loud shouts of, "This is stupid! I want to go back inside."

Jesse hops, skips and runs down the hill, as her kite lifts into the air. "Look at my Barbie kite everybody! Look at how beautiful she is in the air," she shrieks as she runs past her fellow classmates.

Brittany desperately tries to concentrate on her kite while (at the same time) she watches others and tries to make sure that she will not be in their way.

Casey wants to know why she has to run down the hill, what happens if her kite won't fly and exactly how much string she needs to let out to insure proper kite height.

I go to Jacob and run down the hill with him. As soon as we have his kite in the air, he brags that his kite is the highest and the fastest.

Jesse has been running around with high flying Barbie for about twenty minutes. I look up just in time to see her run directly into a tree. No problem! She just keeps holding the string and giggling as she tells her story to her classmates.

I look up on the hill and see Brittany standing there watching below as her classmates fly their kites. I notice something white draped all over her. As I walk closer, I notice that she is tangled in kite string. She cannot move, because the string has her feet bound. I run to her and immediately begin to free her. She notices the panic in my voice and the quick movements that I use to get the string off her. As I lean down and begin to unwind the kite string, Brittany places her hand on my shoulder and says, "It's okay. I knew you would untangle me when you weren't so busy. I didn't mind watching the others while I waited."

Casey's kite rises as it is lifted by gentle breezes. However, it won't remain aloft. She wants to know why it won't stay up, why she has to keep running and isn't it about time to go back to the room?

Just at that moment, I look up at the sky and see it is flecked with all different shapes, colors and sizes of kites. Then, I look around to view my kindergarten class. The "***D***s" are running wildly, and the "***I***s" are giggling and rolling down the hill. The "***S***s" are sitting in the grass making clover chains for me, and the "**C**s" are asking questions. Just like the kites above me, I realize that my students are all special and unique. They decorate my classroom with their differences and varieties.

Even in an activity as playful as flying a kite, ***DISC*** is important. Jacob, the "***D***" student, is excited and optimistic even before the actual kite flying event. His goal is to have the biggest and best kite of all. When he cannot get his kite up into the air, he immediately becomes frustrated, impatient and discouraged. He does not ask the teacher for help. He quits and is ready to go inside. It is Jacob's high "***D***" personality traits (Dominating/Directing) that cause his actions and reactions to the day's events.

Jesse is the happy-go-lucky high "***I***" in the class. She is responding well to the kite flying activity, because it is a fun and favorable outing. She is seeking high praise for her beautiful kite, because approval and popularity are the overwhelming needs that her "***I***" personality demands. With this praise will come the social acceptance that each "***I***" student feels is essential.

The "***S***" of the group, Brittany, is easygoing, agreeable and undemanding. Her softhearted ways are obvious in her desire not to get in the way of the other students. She limits her territory so that her classmates may have more room to fly their kites. Empathy and compassion are two traits of the "***S***" personality. Brittany is aware of the pressure and stress which her teacher is experiencing with all of the students flying kites. Rather than ask her teacher to help her untangle the kite string from around her legs, Brittany passively waits until the teacher notices that she is tangled in her kite string. When Brittany senses that the teacher feels badly for not noticing her tangled situation earlier, Brittany is quick to reassure the teacher that she did not mind being entangled in the string. This is a classic example of the non-demanding and calm nature of the "***S***" personality.

Casey, with her high "***C***" personality, is looking for the structure, order and logic in kite flying. She wants to know all there is to know about the proper way to fly her kite. "Why?" is her biggest question. The experience of flying a kite is not as important to Casey as the desire to fly her kite correctly, efficiently and flawlessly.

Knowing and understanding the principles of ***DISC*** reveal to this teacher that:

"***D***" Jacob needs help to understand that goals are important, but occasional defeats or set-backs are part of life. He needs to learn to be determined and not give up easily. He is an optimistic and confident dreamer. Build on these personality traits.

"***D***": Jacob needs help in learning to ask for assistance. Asking for help is not a sign of weakness but of strength. He is a natural risk-taker, but he fears people taking advantage of him. Build on his self-confident competitiveness.

"***I***": Jesse needs assistance in learning that popularity and praise do not define her self-worth. She fears being ignored, ridiculed or losing social recognition. Since she wants to feel socially accepted, she may make unnecessary compromises in her pursuit of making others happy.

"***I***": Jesse may need help with peer pressure. Because of her overwhelming need to impress, it is easy for Jesse to be drawn into unwise situations. She is too trusting and weak-willed. She is too easily influenced by others. She needs to develop self-reliance and self-discipline.

"***S***": Brittany will need the teacher to help her develop assertiveness with people when appropriate. She is often submissive and shy, even to the point of timidity. She is a reluctant decision-maker, and she prefers listening rather than acting.

"***S***": Brittany responds best to sincere acceptance and appreciation. The teacher needs to provide personal assurances and support. If she doesn't receive these, she may become a fearful spectator, lacking initiative. Brittany doesn't like to be yelled at or to receive sarcasm. Rather, she needs a friendly and appreciative environment that includes support and help.

"***C***": Casey likes tasks which are controlled and precise. The teacher will need to occasionally provide additional reassurance, because some tasks (such as kite flying) do not have an environment that is controlled and precise. He likes consistency and fears the unknown. Casey dislikes sudden changes and interruptions. He prefers to be a careful, cautious, critical thinker.

"***C***": Casey will need the teacher to thoroughly explain all tasks, expectations and requirements, so that he will not worry as much about failure. Casey desires to be accurate and exacting. He is, therefore, logical and orderly, as well as highly organized. Build on this teachableness and natural curiosity and inquisitiveness.

Task: Kite Flying

DISC Plan:

Put "***D***" students in charge of showing and teaching the different ways their classmates might try to fly their kites.

Let "***I***" students do show and tell. Let the class see their flashy kites. Also, you may want to allow them to interview fellow classmates about their adventures and observations of the kite flying experience.

Allow the "***S***" students to write a poem, draw a picture or write a short story describing the kite flying event.

The "***C***" students should be the ones to explain what they learned about the kite flying experience. Let them share the best ways to get kites to fly. Encourage them to provide theories as to the reasons for the ways that worked best.

Popcorn Day

Each year in my third grade class, I look forward to our unit on foods. There are several lessons that involve a real hands-on approach to the different foods that we are discussing for that particular day. Without a doubt, my favorite lesson is "Popcorn Day." I use a strategy that creates an inquisitive atmosphere for my students.

On Popcorn Day, the children come to group time and discover newspapers spread out all over the floor. Blue sheets of paper are laid out to cover the newspapers. In the center of all of the paper is an unknown object placed in a paper bag.

It is during this activity that I can truly see the different personality styles of my students. For example, the high "***D***" students are so eager and anxious. They want to know what is under the paper bag and if they can be the one to uncover it.

When I am certain that I have the attention of my entire class, I explain to the students that we are going to discuss the origin, uses and popping of popcorn. Then I ask, "What makes popcorn pop?" I love all of the different responses.

The high "***I***" students are always so excited. They give creative responses such as, "They pop because they are rubbing up against each other." Then they begin to demonstrate with their bodies how the kernels rub together by jumping and rubbing up against their classmates.

The high "***S***" students will apologize for not knowing the exact answer but immediately let me know they are dying to find out.

Without a doubt, it is the high "***C***" students who are usually the last to respond to the question of how popcorn pops but soon will be the ones who provide a step-by-step explanation.

I lift the paper bag and reveal an old-fashioned popper. I place the children where they can all get a good look. After pouring the oil and popcorn in the base of the popper and plugging it in, I conveniently forget to place the yellow domed lid on the top of the popper. I then step to the side to wash and dry my hands.

One can only imagine what happens next! As the students watch in amazement, the popcorn begins to explode onto the dark blue sheets of paper. I make several halfhearted attempts to cover the explosion, much to no avail. My assistant captures the expressions on film, so that we may go back later and watch ourselves. It is at this time that the uniqueness of each student and all the unique personalities are clearly revealed.

The high "***D***" students are quick to want to take control of the situation. It is interesting to see how the "***D***" students are the first to see that I have left the lid off the popper. The "***D***s" will tell all the students, "Get back while I get the lid. I'm not afraid to cover it. It won't hurt me."

The high "***I***" students are mesmerized by all of the activity. They are the ones laughing and squealing the loudest, with their mouths open wide trying to catch the flying popcorn. The "***I***s" are the ones begging to leave the popper uncovered. "Wow!" the "***I***s" say. "It looks like it is snowing! Look how beautiful. Let's build a popcorn man."

I can always identify the high "***S***" students by the looks of horror on their faces. The lid off the popper, popcorn flying everywhere and their classmates reacting in all different styles and degrees tends to upset the "***S***" students a bit. Once, I even had an "***S***" student tell the class that she felt as if they owed me an apology for laughing at me, because I forgot to put the top on the popper. "It is not nice to laugh at people," she said. "Everyone forgets to do things sometimes. Now, I think we need to tell Mrs. Swanson that we are sorry for laughing at her mistake and help her pick up the popcorn."

While the "***S***" students are horrified, the high "**C**" students are usually disgusted. They remain in the back of the circle and never try to catch the popcorn with their mouths or their hands. I overhear their remarks, and it always makes me chuckle. "She should have known to put the lid on the popper. I would have put the lid on the popper before I even plugged it in," they say. "Look at all the popcorn that she wasted. We could be eating that right now."

After a few minutes, I explain to the students that I meant to leave the lid off the popper, so that they could thoroughly experience the popping of the corn . We share and discuss our observations of the popping of the popcorn and talk about the uses of popcorn.

I do not know if all of my students ever fully appreciate the firsthand experience of the popping process. However, I do know, without a doubt, that they all enjoy the experience of the eating process!

In observing the different actions and reactions of her students, this teacher was able to see ***DISC*** in action:

The high "**D**" students displayed impatience, courage and sometimes recklessness. These students were not afraid to approach the popper and put the lid on it. They did, however, lack a proper plan of action. The attitude, "It won't hurt me," is an example of the high "**D**" attitude of boldness.

The high "***I***" students displayed significant involvement and creativity. They saw the popping corn as a beautiful and exciting thing, and they pleaded for the lid to be left off the popper. The high "***I***" students simply went with the flow and let whatever was going to happen, happen.

The popcorn exploding in the air surprised the high "***S***" students. Because it is difficult for the high "***S***" to quickly adjust to change, this situation was a bit unnerving. These students expected the lid to be on the popper, and when it wasn't, the security of the predictable and friendly environment that they expected suddenly vanished.

The cautious and intense traits of the high "**C**" students were evident in this lesson. Their strong drive to do things correctly and their curious and questioning nature led them to appear to be unsociable and judgmental. Rather than participate and have fun, the high "**C**" students were concentrating on the proper way popcorn should be popped and used.

Knowing and understanding the principles of ***DISC*** reveal to this teacher that:

"***D***" students are impulsive and will frequently begin an assignment without obtaining or fully understanding the directions. They are doers and like to be productive. Encourage them to begin assignments with the proper planning. Give them concise directions.

"***D***" students are focused on results. Getting it done is more important than getting it right. They like doing things the fastest and most efficient way possible. Short-term assignments are better for them, because they allow "***D***s" to work in short bursts of competitive energy.

"***I***" students like the freedom to express themselves. This also includes freedom from details or rigid structure. They can be restless and impulsive. Allow them a little breathing room to be themselves, but guard against their becoming directionless. They need structure. Give them stimulating and fun structure in order to channel their creativity.

"***I***" students are imaginative, and they are adept at expressing their creativity. Since they are sociable and outgoing, allow them small amounts of time to socialize and share. They thrive on interaction.

"***S***" students resist change. They fear and resist change, but they love the status quo. Routine and stability are two of their greatest needs. Prepare them for any deviations from the norm.

"***S***" students desire to give and receive empathetic feedback. Always correct and support them with a sense of "team" (Together Everyone Achieves More). Maintain a friendly and supportive environment. Otherwise, they may become defensive and stubborn.

"***C***" students prefer an environment of procedures and order that result in logical outcomes. They are very analytical and meticulous as they proceed with tasks in a very thorough and orderly fashion. Affirm their need by helping them to bring a sense of logic out of illogical results.

"***C***" students sometimes have a tendency to be complainers with a critical spirit. This can lead to their being cold and insensitive, as well as self-centered. Be quick to help these students find proper and constructive words to express their feelings and needs.

Task: Popping popcorn experiment

DISC Plan:

Allow "***D***" students to be "Popcorn Monitors" making sure that the other students stay safely away from the popper.

Allow the "***I***" students to reenact the popcorn popping through an interpretative dance while they catch flying popcorn in their mouths. This is an experience they will never forget!

Allow the "***S***" students to take the pictures, record the remarks and serve the popcorn.

Allow the "**C**" students to create a step-by-step chart showing how to pop popcorn correctly, as well as how to pop popcorn incorrectly. Also, they could demonstrate ways popcorn can be turned into caramel corn or strung together to become a decoration or other uses for popcorn.

What Page *Are* We On?

The first day that we have reading groups is always an exciting day for my first graders. Since I had explained several days earlier what we would be doing in these groups, my children were very excited. I, too, was excited. I had carefully mapped out a precise lesson plan that would have the children quietly listening to the story and then answering questions and discussing the events of the story in an organized manner. It did not take long to realize that my lesson plan was not designed to work well with the various personality styles of my students.

The "**D**" child, Matthew, demanded to be the first one to read. By the time I arrived at the reading circle, Matthew had already picked out who would read after him, what part of the story that person would read and who would read after that! In addition, Matthew had arranged the seating chart of the reading circle and was telling the other children where to sit. During the reading time, Matthew finished his turn and was ready to proceed to something else more challenging. "Can I get another book and read it?" he asked, interrupting me as

I read aloud. Clearly, Matthew was the dominant personality in this group.

One of the "***I***" type children, Mary, was busy talking to her friends and wanted to be sure she got to sit by them. At first, she did not even open her book. She was much too concerned with making sure she had greeted the rest of her friends in the circle. The other "***I***" type child, Jonathan, did not even bother to come to the reading group circle. He was visiting the other children who were doing seat work outside of the circle. When I asked him why he had not come to the circle, he said, "I don't know why I have to come. I can't read."

The "***S***" children, Elizabeth and Seth, were very quiet and doing exactly what I had asked them to do. They were seated and waiting patiently with their books opened to the first page of the story that we were about to read. Their eyes were focused on me as they waited for me to begin.

The "***C***" children, Emily and John, asked several questions before and during the reading group. "Is this the right book?" "What page are we on?" "Can I take this book home tonight?" "Are we going to get a grade on this?" Their questions were coming at me faster than I could answer them.

It was clearly evident to me that there was more to a reading group than all of us just being on the same page at the same time.

The ***DISC*** Model of Human Behavior is easily illustrated by this classroom reading group.

Matthew, with a "***D***" type personality, is both active and task-oriented. He is a Dominating/ Directing student, as is evident with his take-charge attitude during the reading circle activity. "***D***" students will loudly and aggressively declare their disapproval when things do not go their way or if they become restless. Matthew's interrupting pleas to be allowed to proceed to something else after he had finished reading his part is an example of the impatience that "***D***" students often exhibit.

Every teacher or parent is able to recognize an "***I***" student and to recall examples of "***I***" children. Mary and Jonathan are the Interactive/Influencing students who are so lively! They want to have something going on every minute. They are talkative, open and optimistic. Creative ideas abound in them, but they are often unfocused in carrying them out because of their short attention spans.

Elizabeth and Seth, the "***S***" type personalities, are the Steady/Stable students. They are the good listeners and peacemakers. As Elizabeth and Seth demonstrate, they are the ones who always follow directions. The "***S***" student rarely shows visible signs of anger, excitement or enthusiasm.

The "***C***" in the ***DISC*** Model of Human Behavior represents the Cautious/Compliant student. Emily and John are intent on doing the right thing. They ask questions that are designed to gain information on how, when, where and especially why something should be done. After "***C***" students, such as Emily and John, have their questions answered, they become less apprehensive and can then begin to focus on the task at hand.

This teacher quickly learned the different personalities she had in her reading group and even more importantly, learned that we are never all on the same page.

Knowing and understanding the principles of ***DISC*** reveal to this teacher that:

"***D***": Matthew's need for control is not an option but a driving force in his life. The teacher needs to provide him with opportunities that will allow him to be in charge and feel a sense of ownership. He likes to direct and to lead. Let him be a dominant director.

"***D***": Matthew will always say what he thinks. He will be blunt and straightforward, as well as inconsiderate, sarcastic and abrasive. He is not intentionally trying to hurt anyone and therefore, needs guidance and correction without anger.

"***I***": Mary and Jonathan respond best to a fun-filled environment. They like to make everything fun and flashy. A teacher should realize that with "***I***" students, constant encouragement is the key to building upon their upbeat enthusiasm. Keep it positive.

"***I***": Mary and Jonathan's teacher needs to always consider and affirm their need for social interaction and recognition. They are people people. They love to be personable and talkative with others. They are interesting and interested.

"***S***": Elizabeth and Seth are not natural leaders or talkers. They are listeners. The teacher should never make the mistake of forcing them to take leadership positions. They don't like being pushed into situations. Under this type of pressure, Elizabeth and Seth become hesitant and indecisive. The teacher needs to build on their natural desire to serve.

"***S***": Elizabeth and Seth are rarely troublemakers. Their cooperation many times results from a fear of confrontation and conflict. They are amiable and gentle and are the sweetest people in the world. They love peace and pleasantness. The teacher should encourage them to be expressive with their feelings rather than being passive.

"***C***": Emily and John are perfectionists. Their need to ask questions does not stem from poor listening skills but rather from a desire to meet their high standards. Never tell "**C**" students that they are too picky. If you do, this will devalue their entire approach to life.

"***C***": Emily and John need reassurance. The teacher should provide situations that will affirm a high "**C**'s" value as a person. Remember that "**C**s" cherish excellence and high quality. Reaffirm their sense of self-sacrifice, consistency and competence.

Task: Classroom reading group – reading out loud. Ask the students specific questions regarding the content of what they have read, and let them express their unique perspectives and opinions.

DISC Plan:

Allow "***D***" students to call the reading group together and arrange the room. Also, let the "***D***" students notify the group of page turnings, or let them turn the page for the teacher.

Assign "***I***" students reading portions to act out. Let them bring the characters to life.

Assign "***S***" students the task of listening for their favorite part of the story and deciding which character they liked the most and why.

Assign "***C***" students the task of asking questions to be used in group discussion.

Eraser "Snort Out"

It was my first year to teach first grade. One can only imagine how I felt. My nerves were on edge, and I felt like crawling into a shell and not coming out until June. To my pleasant surprise, my first week of school went smoothly. I learned all of my students' names, and I hugged and nurtured all of them until I believed that each one felt as if our classroom was his second home.

By the second week, I was not only calmer and more confident, but I also found myself enthusiastic and excited about the wonderful year ahead. One day as I was teaching about the weather, I noticed that one of the little girls had raised her hand. It was Lane, my high "***I***" student. When she wasn't talking, she was wiggling and squirming. I noticed, however, that on this particular day, she was not doing any of those things. Instead, she was sitting quietly, and her right index finger was pointed at her nose. Her unusual calmness scared me. I quickly asked, "Lane, what is the matter?"

With the utmost caution, she replied, "I-I-I have an eraser stuck up my nose."

I looked closer and, sure enough, she had lodged a strip of an eraser halfway up one of her nostrils. Immediately, I broke into a cold sweat and wondered how I was going to handle this situation. Before I even had time to formulate a possible solution, my students were handling the situation individually.

Kyle, the high "***D***" of the group, was the first to speak. He was full of advice and ready to give it freely. "Well, that was a stupid thing to do! You better send her to the principal's office." Then Kyle continued in his domineering manner, "No, maybe she needs to go to the clinic." He was beside himself and ready to spring into action. I knew I had to do something quickly, or I would soon have more than one problem on my hands!

Lindsay and Bart, the high "***I***s" in the class, became very excited over this turn of events. Learning about the weather seemed inconsequential when there was a child with an eraser up her nose! Lindsay and Bart certainly were not going to miss this opportunity. Both of them quickly moved next to Lane and began joking and laughing. I started to see Lane relax a bit, but I was still in a panic.

James, the "***C***" of the group, was working on a plan to get the eraser out of Lane's nose. He had assessed the situation, calculated the risks and was well on his way to his own unique "scientific" step-by-step plan of extraction. James made his way to the chalkboard and began drawing out a detailed diagram of what I needed to do to get the eraser out of Lane's nose.

As I looked around the room, I noticed Cecelia, the "***S***" of our class, sitting in back of Lane. Cecelia had her hand on Lane's shoulder and was patting her in a gentle manner. Every once in a while, she would lean forward and softly whisper to Lane that everything was going to be okay.

I somehow managed to get control of myself as I walked over to Lane's desk. "Lane, these may be the most important words that you will hear Mrs. Barton say to you this year. Whatever you do, don't snort in. You have to snort out." With those directions, Lane did just that. The eraser flew into the air with great force. It traveled across the room and landed with a bounce on the floor.

All of the children watched with amazement, and then, in unison, they responded with, "O-o-o-o-o."

It took a little while for all of us to calm down and regain our composure. Once we did, I returned to the subject of the weather, as a much wiser and confident teacher.

All educators know that unexpected situations usually arise at the worst possible times. Knowing ***DISC*** can actually give a teacher the advantage of knowing how certain individual students and the class, as a whole, will react.

Kyle, with his "***D***" personality traits, was the one to immediately step up to the plate and offer several suggestions as to what needed to be done. He was not at all concerned about what others would think of his ideas.

Lindsay and Bart, the "***I***s", saw this unexpected turn of events as just another opportunity to have some fun, and they quickly capitalized on it. Let us also not forget that it was an "***I***" who got the eraser up her nose in the first place!

The "***S***", Cecelia, was so sweet and kindhearted. Her main concern was making sure that Lane was comforted and calmed.

The high "***C***" traits of James were evident in his thorough assessment of the situation and his calculated development of a procedure to remove the eraser from Lane's nose.

With the knowledge of ***DISC***, this teacher was able to see that her students were using their primary personality traits to solve a problem rather than create more chaos. Knowing ***DISC*** can give a teacher the insights with which to handle unexpected situations in the classroom in an effective manner.

Knowing and understanding the principles of ***DISC*** reveal to this teacher that:

"***D***": Kyle is invigorated by pressure situations and will usually be the first one to react. He is diligent and industrious, and he is able to complete an amazing amount of work. He thrives on hard work, even under pressure.

"***D***": Kyle is not afraid to stand alone and voice his opinions, even when others do not agree with him. He is independent, courageous and confident. He may carry these even to the point of defiance.

"***I***": Lindsay and Bart are optimistic. They can see the good (and fun) in any situation. They are enthusiastic and inspiring.

"***I***": Lindsay and Bart have a need to be at the center of the action and attention. They have charming and magnetic personality styles. They love feeling important and are always on the go.

"***S***": Cecelia is supportive and helpful in quiet, reassuring ways. She is motivated by helping others. She is a loyal, trustworthy and faithful friend.

"***S***": Empathy is a strong, driving force in Cecelia's interaction with others. She is softhearted. She is kind, patient and understanding.

"***C***": James is hesitant to react or offer any assistance, because he must analyze the facts of the situation first. He is overly cautious and contemplative. He feels responsible for his actions. At times, he may prefer solitude.

"***C***": James does not do well when put in pressure-filled situations that require quick thinking. He is conscientious and questioning and wants to do things the right way.

Situation: Classroom crises that require the teacher's undivided and immediate attention.

DISC Plan:

Allow the "***D***" students to go for help, get supplies or monitor the class.

Allow the "***I***" students to lead in a class activity or read to the rest of the class, so that the teacher may handle the situation.

Allow the "***S***" students to talk or spend time with those involved in the situation as a means to calm, support and encourage.

Allow the "***C***" students to help formulate a plan to use during future emergency situations like a fire drill or tornado drill.

The Lost Money

Every fall our school has a book fair. This book fair is a fund-raiser that provides students with the opportunity to buy books and then gives a percentage of the proceeds to the school.

Shelves of shiny, new books for kids of all ages line the halls. The students are encouraged to browse before school starts in the morning. One day out of the week, each class gets to go to the book fair and buy books.

When my fourth grade class had the opportunity to go and purchase books, everyone lined up anxiously. They were all excited, especially Virginia, an "***S***". Virginia loves to read. She knows exactly what she likes and what she wants.

Eagerly, Virginia reached into her desk to get her five dollars, but she couldn't find it anywhere. In a panicked voice, Virginia said, "I can't find my money! I've lost my money!" She started sobbing profusely.

Allan, a "***D***" personality, immediately spoke up in a bossy tone, "Hurry up! Okay, whoever has Virginia's money or knows where it is, give it back RIGHT NOW so that we can go!" Virginia sobbed louder.

Jessica, an "***I***" personality, put her arm around Virginia and said, "It's okay, Virginia. Your money will show up. Come on and go with me. We'll have fun anyway. Let's play together at recess." Virginia nodded her head and smiled a faint smile.

Dustin, David and Tiffany, all "***S***" students, crowded around Virginia. Dustin told her how sorry he was that her money was gone, and David offered to share his money with her.

Tiffany offered her a tissue to wipe her tears and told her that she would help her look for it.

Meanwhile, Josh, a "***C***" student, was full of helpful instructions and questions. "Virginia," he said, "clean out your desk and look real good. Look through everything – your books and notebook. Clean out your backpack and check your pockets. Think real hard. When was the last time that you saw your five dollars? What did you have it in? Where have you been?" Virginia was trying very hard to keep up with his instructions and questions, but her frustration was building.

Virginia had a lot of help and support from her classmates. All of them pulled together in their own special way and came to Virginia's side. Yes, Virginia did find her five dollars. It had been turned in at the book fair. Evidently, she had dropped it earlier that morning.

It was so inspiring to watch how all of the personality types reached out to help one of their classmates in need. How nice it would be if our world had such a caring and serving spirit. How beautiful it would be if we could all work together in unity for a common cause.

This crisis situation gave the teacher an insight into the workings of ***DISC***.

Allan, the "***D***", immediately called for the person who took the money to give it back. He was direct and demanding.

Jessica, the "***I***", tried to calm Virginia and help take her mind off of her problem by promising a fun time at recess.

Dustin, David and Tiffany, the "***S***" personalities, all supported Virginia. They let her know that they cared.

Josh, the "*C*", used his ability to analyze and break down things to help Virginia think through what she had done, so that she could trace her lost money. In his own way, Josh was compassionate and helpful.

Knowing and understanding the principles of ***DISC*** reveal to this teacher:

"*D*": Allan gets to the main point quickly. He is goal-oriented. He is to the point and direct.

"*D*": Allan focuses on action-based results. He is decisive and likes challenges.

"*D*": Danger: Allan can become abrasive, dogmatic and demanding. He can run roughshod over people.

"*I*": Jessica focuses on fun times. She is gregarious and likes making others happy in her carefree way.

"*I*": Jessica is optimistic and tends to see things through rose-colored glasses. She thinks everything is super and rosy.

"*I*": Danger: Jessica can become unrealistic and can be easily manipulated.

"*S*": Dustin, David and Tiffany are supportive in sincere ways. They have sweet dispositions and are good listeners.

"*S*": Dustin, David and Tiffany are supportive in a crisis. They are steady and dependable stabilizers.

"*S*":Danger: They can become inflexible and resistant to change. They may even become resentful.

"*C*": Josh is analytical and careful. He is cautious and a precise perfectionist.

"*C*": Josh is sensitive and helpful. He seeks to be diplomatic.

"*C*": Danger: Josh may become too critical and rigid, because he relies on his feelings, rather than seeing the big picture.

Task: Problem Solving Activities
DISC Plan:
Allow "***D***" students to generate "***what***" questions.
Allow "***I***" students to generate "***who***" questions.
Allow "***S***" students to generate "***how***" questions.
Allow "***C***" students to generate "***why***" questions.

Bubba – A Product of Democracy

Fourth grade! What an age! The students are too young to know it all but are old enough to know a little something about everything. Fourth grade, I believe, is a perfect age to introduce democracy and the process of democratic decision making. I couldn't think of a better way to teach my students the process of democracy than with the decision we had to make regarding the possibility of adopting a classroom pet. I thought that this would be a fun learning experience that would instill in each student a lesson in cooperation and teamwork.

I began with a casual hint that as part of our science curriculum, we might want to consider having our own classroom pet. I suggested a few guidelines as to appropriate size, cost, survival and care of the animal.

Quickly, Meredith, my high "***I***" student, shouted out, "I know! I know what we can do!" She clapped her hands with excitement. "This will be so much fun. Let's all write our favorite pet down on a piece of paper, and then fold it up real little. Then, we'll put all of the pieces in a box, blindfold someone, and let him pull a piece of paper from the box." With that suggestion, Meredith plopped down beside her desk and frantically began her search for a box. "I know there is a box in my desk. I remember seeing one," she said as she pulled the contents of her desk onto the floor. I could not imagine where all of this stuff came from, considering it was only the first week of school.

Within minutes, Walker, my "***C***" student, chimed in matter-of-factly, "Definitely NOT a good idea." Once he had our attention, he continued with a worried tone of voice, "What if someone wants a dog? We can't have a dog in here! Or what about rabbits? My dad says rabbits have babies fast. Then what would we do with all the babies? Or, worse, cats! I'm allergic to cats! I think we should think about this tonight and tomorrow morning. Then let's make a list of animals to adopt. We can choose two people to count the votes so that we make sure that we counted them correctly and..."

Meredith, from her position on the floor, replied, "That way is no fun. What do you think we should do, Hope?"

Hope, my high "***S***" student, turned a ghostly shade of white and slowly looked around the room at the fifteen students staring intently at her. "I don't know," she said hesitantly. Both Meredith and Walker sighed deeply at Hope's uncommitted response.

Ty, a high "***C***", spoke up. "I think we should do whatever Walker said. We can all think about our choice of a pet tonight." Ty's words were met with about as many "yeas" as "nays."

Amid the hum of all the students trying to talk at once came a loud and stern voice. Clay said, "This is dumb! Tomorrow I'm bringing my hamster. My mom hates him anyway, and I am sick of having to clean his cage all of the time. We can set his cage right there," he said, as he pointed to the shelf behind him. Clay continued, "He is cute and small and furry, and you'll love him. His name is Bubba."

No one spoke another word about adopting a pet as Clay had seemingly made the decision for us all. Bubba came to our classroom the next day and was a happy little hamster.

The students realized that they had a lot to learn about caring for a pet, and I learned we had a lot to learn about the democratic process!

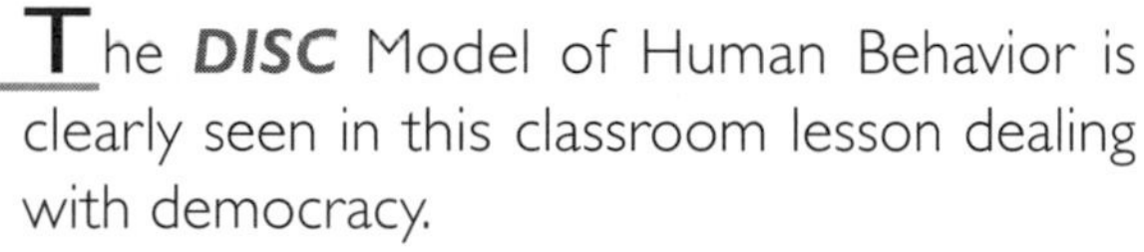

The ***DISC*** Model of Human Behavior is clearly seen in this classroom lesson dealing with democracy.

Clay, the "***D***" in the classroom, grows impatient with the discussion on the proper way to adopt a pet. He simply wants to get to the end result. He is decisive and believes the end justifies the means.

Meredith, the "***I***" in the classroom, sees this lesson as an opportunity to have fun and be creative. She is excited and enthusiastic about this lesson, but her inability to find the box amid all of her clutter impedes the progress of her plan.

Hope, the "***S***" in the classroom, is quick to come to Meredith's aid. She is easily motivated by Meredith's enthusiasm and wants to help her find the box. However, when Hope is asked to make a choice, she does not take a stand. She simply wants everyone to be happy.

Walter, the "***C***" in the classroom, is more interested in the process than the product. He wants time to gather the facts and reason through the various choices before making a decision.

Knowing and understanding the principles of ***DISC*** reveal to the teacher that:

"***D***": Clay grew impatient with the continued discussions. "***D***" students do not like to move slowly or talk without producing results. They are productive doers and like activity. They dislike indecision and laziness. They are results-oriented.

"***D***": Clay was correct in reasoning that a hamster was a perfect pet for the classroom. "***D***" students are practical. They like having choices. They get to the point quickly, decisively and directly.

"***I***": Meredith's enthusiasm at the suggestion of a classroom pet was overwhelming. "***I***" students are easily excited. They can be impulsive, and they like a lot of interesting and stimulating activities.

"***I***": The clutter and mess underneath Meredith's desk is indicative of the lack of organizational skills that characterize most "***I***" students. They are great starters but poor finishers. This is often the result of being unfocused and undisciplined.

"***S***": Hope recognized Meredith's need for help and quickly went to her aid. "***S***" students are intuitive, empathetic and supportive. They are motivated by helping, and they love to be of service to others. This will help them to feel appreciated.

"***S***": When asked to decide between the two ideas, Hope would not choose. "***S***" students are fearful of causing disharmony. They are submissive and cooperative. They have a sweet disposition. They are easily compatible with others.

"***C***": Walter was quick to criticize Meredith's idea. "***C***" students can be critical and judgmental. They can be self-centered, calculating and unsociable. They need to learn to work together with others.

"***C***": Walter wants time to think through his choices before suggesting a possible classroom pet. "***C***" students are thorough and analytical. These students tend to be careful and cognitive. They are perfectionists.

Task: Class consensus

DISC Plan:

Allow "***D***" students to write suggestions on the board regarding possible project topics.

Allow "***I***" students to decide the method of voting and lead the class by having a say in the process.

Allow "***S***" students to work in teams, count the votes and announce the "winning" idea.

Allow "***C***" students to discuss the pros and cons of the recorded suggestions.

The Red Chair

As with all teachers, discipline was a top priority with me as I began my second year teaching fifth grade. I decided that I would place a chair outside my door, and when a student was misbehaving, he would be sent outside of the classroom to sit in the chair. The principal of our school, Mr. Smith, liked to walk up and down the halls throughout the day. So the chance of Mr. Smith seeing a student sitting in the chair was great, and the chance of being invited to his office was even greater! It only took two weeks for the chair to gain a reputation, and before long, students spoke of the red chair with dread.

The red chair became the ultimate form of punishment and was to be avoided at all costs. Knowing, however, that there were different personality styles in the classroom, I knew that someone would, sooner or later, give in to temptation, and the chair would eventually be used.

Rob, the high "***I***" of the class, was the first to be sent to the red chair. One day his continuous classroom antics had tried my patience to the point that I sternly told him to seat himself in the red chair. Every child in the room gasped at the mere mention of the red chair. A deafening silence fell on the room. Even I felt the tension and seriousness of the situation. But Rob did not. He made some sort of a joke about getting the prize for being the first one to be sent to the red chair, and he nonchalantly walked out the door.

Several minutes later, I heard talking and laughing outside of the door. I quickly walked to the door knowing that I would probably catch Rob joking with a fellow student. To my surprise, when I threw the door open, I discovered Mr. Smith and Rob joking and laughing like two old friends. Mr. Smith began to share with me the funny joke Rob had told him, and the two broke out in laughter once again. It certainly was not the form of discipline I had in mind for Rob. Mr. Smith had to be told that Rob was being punished. He had not won a contest.

Several days later Catherine, a high "***D***", called a fellow classmate "a stupid moron." This remark got her a free ticket to the red chair. As she walked out of the classroom, I heard her say, "I believe Mr. Smith is out of the building today. It's my lucky day." It was not her lucky day, as Mr. Smith walked by only seconds after Catherine sat down in the red chair. The excuse she had prepared for why she called Sabrina "stupid" was so dynamic and was delivered with such confidence to Mr. Smith, that even I began to believe her innocence for a minute.

Ryan, the "**C**" student of our bunch, continued to debate the worthiness of his favorite baseball team long after I had told him to begin his class work. After several times of disobeying my directions, I sent him to the red chair. My request, however, started a whole new debate. Ryan began with "Who? Me? What did I do? Are you sure it was me? It wasn't me. What was I doing wrong? How long am I going to have to sit there?" It was almost worth telling him to just forget it so that he would stop asking questions!

The day Franklin received his walking papers to the red chair is a day I will not soon forget. Franklin, a high "***S***", was devastated. My heart broke into pieces as he made his way to the door. There were tears in his eyes, as he profusely apologized for his mistake and assured me that it would never happen again.

The red chair successfully remained a part of my discipline plan for many years. I do not know if the students actually learned a great deal from the threat of the red chair, but I know I sure did.

The ***DISC*** Model of Human Behavior is revealed to this teacher through the different ways each student reacts to discipline.

Catherine, the "***D***" in the classroom, approaches the red chair with a defiant attitude. She is determined to control the situation, no matter what.

Rob, the "***I***" in the classroom, approaches the red chair with humor and optimism. He simply sees the red chair as a change of scenery.

Franklin, the "***S***" in the classroom, approaches the red chair with remorse and dread. He feels ashamed and disappointed in himself.

Ryan, the "***C***" in the classroom, approaches the red chair with caution and skepticism. He wants to know his punishment is justified before moving a step.

Knowing and understanding the principles of ***DISC*** reveal to the teacher that:

"***D***": Catherine will try to manipulate or control situations. "***D***" students can be crafty and sly due to the insensitive and inconsiderate side of their nature. This may even go to such extremes as being cold and cruel.

"***D***": When under pressure, Catherine often becomes rebellious and stubborn. "***D***" students fear losing control. They don't like taking orders from others; they want to do things their own way.

"***I***": Rob tries to make a game out of serious situations. "***I***" students want to always look good and "save face." Their playfulness and concern for approval are often associated with stress reduction. "***I***s" definitely prefer humor and entertainment.

"***I***": Rob avoids strict punishment from the principal. "***I***" students are "people persons." Their warm and personable demeanor many times overshadows their weaknesses. "***I***s" are very outgoing, and they seek to avoid conflict or confrontation. They often perceive life according to their feelings.

"***S***": Franklin accepts his punishment humbly. "***S***" students are submissive and like to cooperate with others. They can be very accepting and overly sensitive.

"***S***": Franklin is hurt and disappointed in his actions. "***S***" students strive to maintain the status quo and keep the peace. They are relaxed and passive, as well as calm and easygoing.

"***C***": Ryan questions the validity of the punishment. "***C***" students become picky and faultfinding when under pressure due to their headstrong, critical and obstinate traits.

"***C***": Ryan wants to understand the nature of the punishment. He needs to know priorities, process and purposes. "***C***" students need to understand, in advance, as many of the aspects and expectations of a situation as possible because of their structured and systematic need and desire for precision.

Task: Discipline
DISC Plan:
When disciplining:
"***D***" students: Establish and remind them that you are the authority in charge.
"***I***" students: Show how poor behavior makes them look bad. Relate popularity to responsibility.
"***S***" students: Show heartfelt, sincere hurt. Explain to them how their behavior contributed to the problem. Also, explain to them that you are not displeased with them as a person, only with their actions.
"***C***" students: Give thorough explanations regarding the reasons for the course of action you take.

What a Trip!

Little did I know that when I walked into my sixth grade classroom on the first day of school, I would be facing two "***D***" type personalities, four "***D/I***" type personalities, seven "***I***" type personalities, five "***S***" type personalities and one "***C***" type personality. Looking back, if I had known then what I know now about personality styles, I would have thought seriously about running away as fast as I could or driving to the nearest unemployment agency.

Fortunately, I did neither. However, little did I realize that because I did not know how to work correctly with different personality types, I would have a difficult year. To survive this year, I would have to take Tagamet daily, use hair color monthly and request prayer from anyone who would listen.

Early in the year, I planned an exciting field trip for our class. We were going to visit the Wood Magic Science Fair located on the Mississippi State University campus. It promised to be a fun and educational experience.

After only ten minutes into the two-hour bus trip, Scott complained, "What time will we get there? Are you sure the bus has enough gas to get to Starkville and back? What's that clicking sound coming from the motor? Don't you hear it? Do you think the bus driver is driving too fast? If he is, we'll get stopped for speeding, and the school could get in an awful lot of trouble. My parents wouldn't like it either."

Once we arrived, the students were eager to begin the tour. Throughout the day, Terri, my "***D***" type student, related her thoughts loudly and often. I heard such comments as, "Don't just stand there. Get out of my way. You don't even know what you're doing. Let me go first. I know where to go and what to do. Couldn't they do better than this? This pizza is terrible. I wish I'd brought my own lunch. Hey look, our teacher is wearing a new dress. She finally made it to the nineties!"

After lunch, we made our way to one of the demonstration booths. The instructor at the booth drew two lines on a white sheet of paper. The pens he used to draw the lines contained two different kinds of ink that attracted termites. He, then, poured approximately one hundred termites from a jar onto the paper, so that we could observe which trail the termites took. He encouraged the students to move toward the table for a closer look.

I noticed that Zack, my "***I***" type student, had a twinkle in his eye as he hurried to the table. He took a deep breath, lowered himself to the paper and blew with all his might. For a brief second, the air was black as termites flew everywhere. Zack doubled over with laughter as he yelled, "Hey, did y'all see how far I blew 'em? Look! They're even in Chrissy's hair!"

Our day came to an end, and we were on our way back to school. I was trying to recover from the activities of the day when I felt a hand on my shoulder. Then I heard Raney, my "***S***" type student, say in her sweet voice, "Would you like for me to massage your shoulders? You seem a little stressed out, and it will make you feel better. Did you know that you are my favorite teacher? Thank you for taking us on the field trip. I had such a good time. I am going to bring you some flowers tomorrow."

I sat quietly and reflected on the day's events. Then I thought about what the next one hundred and sixty-eight days of the year had in store for me with this group of students. Scott interrupted my thoughts. "Do you think it's wise to be taking that many Tagamets at one time?"

By understanding the ***DISC*** Model of Human Behavior, this teacher could have had early insights into her particular students and the different responses that could be expected from different activities, such as a field trip experience.

Terri exhibited the traits common to that of a "***D***" personality. When disappointed or frustrated, she voiced her opinions in a blunt manner that appeared to be cruel and sarcastic. She displayed confidence in knowing where to go and what to do. She had a strong desire to be the leader.

Zack's desire to be the center of attention and to make

people laugh is consistent with that of an "***I***" personality. His impulsive nature and weakness in thinking things through was evident with his "blowing termites" practical joke. Zack's actions were not intended to be malicious or disruptive; they were intended to be entertaining.

Raney's "***S***" personality traits were displayed through her sincere concern for the teacher. Her desire to help the teacher relax and her appreciation for the field trip are just the sweet and supportive actions demonstrated by an "***S***" personality.

Scott, the "***C***" personality, was full of questions. He wanted to make sure that everything was perfect for the field trip. It is his ability to provide close analysis and his desire for perfection, that leads Scott to ask so many questions. He is naturally curious and cautious.

Knowing and understanding the principles of ***DISC*** reveal to this teacher that:

"***D***" students are confident. It is their confidence that fuels their desire to be in charge and to have a position of leadership. They are good administrators but can err on the side of being dictatorial, manipulative and controlling.

"***D***" students are straightforward. They often speak before they think. Unfortunately, that sometimes can make them appear to be harsh. They can be forceful and opinionated. They like to state their thoughts instead of listening to others and asking the opinions of others.

"***I***" students are spontaneous and playful, even to the extent of being undisciplined. They have the ability to seize a moment and make it work to their advantage. They want to be "the show" and have others notice them.

"***I***" students have a need for self-discipline. Sometimes their desire for too much fun, or inappropriate fun, can be self-defeating. They are weak-willed. They must learn to prioritize activities and use time management. They must learn follow-through skills and to complete tasks.

"***S***" students are relaxed, easygoing, calm and pleasant.

"***S***" students can be overly accommodating in their desire to please and to be supportive. They are flexible and adaptive in their quest to be compatible. Sometimes they need to learn to stand up for themselves.

"**C**" students are curious and intense in their quest for perfection. They are detail-oriented, and they are more concerned with quality than with quantity.

"**C**" students sometimes tend to worry too much about things being perfect. Their idealism can create a need for them to ease up a bit and to avoid dwelling on mistakes.

Task: Field Trip

DISC Plan:

Allow "***D***" students a turn to be the captain of a tour group.

Allow "***I***" students enough time to "entertain" and have fun on the ride to and from the field trip.

Allow "***S***" students opportunities to help with administrative duties on the field trip, and then recognize and appreciate their support.

Allow "**C**" students to analyze and evaluate the field trip. Ask them for suggestions for improvements for future trips.

The Secret Pal

Once a week, I choose four students in my seventh grade class to present a show and tell. One particular Friday, our class had a show and tell that I will never forget.

Friday was Michael's day to share something that he had brought from home. Michael was a high "***I***", and everyone liked him. When I called his name, it was obvious from the look on his face that he had forgotten that it was his day to share. Did that stop him? Oh no!

He thought for a second. Then he quickly got up from his desk and moved to the front of the classroom. With wide-eyed excitement, he said, "I have a secret pet. He's in my pocket, and I'll show him to you. You can pet him if you want to." He had the attention of every student as he put his hand in his pocket and pulled out a small paper clip.

I sat at my desk and wondered how the rest of the class was going to react to this idea. Michael walked over to Samantha, a high "***S***", held out his hand ever so carefully, and proudly showed her his pet. He said, "Go ahead and pet it. It won't hurt you. He likes attention."

Samantha actually reached up and gingerly touched the paper clip and said, "He's nice."

As Michael proceeded around the room, several more students petted the paper clip. Then Michael got to David, a high "***C***". David carefully studied the "pet" in Michael's hand and then asked, "What did you say this is? Where did you get it? Do you really think it is a pet?" David did not touch it.

As Michael neared the end of the last row, he got to John. John, a high "***D***", had been waiting impatiently and was anxious to see the small pet up close. He looked at it with a quick glance and said, "Are you crazy? That is not a pet! That is a dumb paper clip!" He was exasperated that Michael had tried to fool the class.

John's comments had no affect on Michael. He was beaming from ear to ear as he took his seat. He was just happy to have a turn in the spotlight.

An hour later, as the class was lining up for recess, Michael called me aside and whispered, "I've been feeding my pet in my pocket, and he's growing. I'll show you." With that, he reached in his pocket and pulled out a larger paper clip. Naturally, he showed everyone else in the class while they were outside at recess. He thought it was all great fun.

The ***DISC*** Model of Human Behavior is illustrated in the "show and tell" exercise of the students.

Jonathan, a high "***D***", did not participate in Michael's fun. Instead, he let Michael know that he was not amused, and that he thought it was dumb.

Michael, a high "***I***", was creative and spontaneous. He had fun and created excitement for the whole class.

Samantha, a high "***S***", was nice and kind to Michael and his pet. She was willing to play along and have fun.

David, a high "***C***", was full of questions that helped him to analyze the situation. Then he drew the valid conclusion that the pet was simply a paper clip.

"***D***": Jonathan deals with concrete facts. He did not want to be treated like he was dumb. Jonathan is quite deliberate and decisive. He tends to ask "**what**" questions rather than "**how**" or "**why**" questions.

"***D***": Jonathan needs statements supported with credibility. He is very straightforward and likes to be convinced. His reasoning is often displayed in his need for concise data.

"***I***": Michael is quick thinking and witty. He is very lively, expressive and enjoys bouncing ideas off of others.

"***I***": Michael is fun and entertaining to watch. He is an entertainer who thrives on applause and attention. He enjoys being the class clown and making people laugh.

"***S***": Samantha is agreeable and non-threatening. She is amiable and acts non-aggressively. She is very faithful and loyal.

"***S***": Samantha enjoys people having fun, and she likes a casual and friendly atmosphere. She can be very self-sacrificing in her quest for participation.

"***C***": David does not like silliness. He is very serious and conservative by nature.

"***C***": David likes quality work validated by credibility. He desires feedback from others and wants others to notice the correctness and precision of his work. David dislikes personal criticism of his work efforts by either his colleagues or his superiors.

Task: Show and Tell

DISC Plan:

Encourage "***D***" students to relax and expand their imaginations. They need to join the class fun and develop a less serious outlook on life.

Encourage "***I***" students to use their creativity by acknowledging what they accomplish, rather than pointing out how poorly they did. Since they thrive on attention, give them credit or praise publicly, when appropriate.

Encourage "***S***" students to break away from the routine and be creative. They need to vary their activities and not be afraid to try new things.

Encourage "***C***" students to use their intuition to think of new ways to create new ideas. They also need to listen to the suggestions and varied points of view of others.

Research Nightmares

As someone who enjoys finding out about various things and passing that information on to others, I thought it would be enlightening to have my eighth grade students complete a research paper. I began in July preparing my research paper lesson plans. I compiled a list of suggested topics, a schedule showing when each item was due, a sample research paper (both typed and handwritten) and other specific requirements of the paper. I knew that I had covered my bases and was ready for the research paper assignment. I felt sure that I had prepared for everything, and that there could not be any questions from the students.

The Tuesday after Labor Day, I began to explain the handouts for the research assignment. As I was going through the list of suggested topics, my "***I***" student, Tamara, raised her hand. She began waving her hand and bouncing around in her seat so much that I finally called on her. "Can I do my paper on ostriches? We own an ostrich farm, and I can get lots of information. Are we going to present these in class? If we do, can I bring in an ostrich feather and egg to show the class? Oh! Oh! I have a great idea. We can take a field trip out to our farm. I can present my report there, and everyone can see an ostrich up close. It would be so much fun! Can we, please, please?" (At that point, I was just grateful that she had not mentioned bringing an ostrich to class!)

I explained that the research paper would be presented in class. She could bring her egg and feather to class, and I would think about the field trip. Then I continued with my lesson, only to be interrupted by Owen, my high "***D***" student. "Do we have to follow this schedule of events, or can we turn in each thing early? If you approve my topic today, I'll go to the library tonight, so I can get the books I need. Is it all right if I turn it all in early? I can research it, write it and turn it in by the end of next week."

I explained to Owen that I wanted to stick to the schedule. I overheard Autumn, my high "***S***" student, turn to Owen and ask, in a quiet voice, "Why do you want to be in such a hurry? Take your time and do a really good job. That way, you will make Mrs. Jones proud of you."

The bell dismissed the students, and I noticed that Kacy, my "***C***" student, was lingering behind. She approached me and asked, "Are you going over these handouts again tomorrow? I want to make sure that I understand everything. I took notes, made a list of my top three choices and numbered them by preference and difficulty level. I will look over them tonight and come to a decision by tomorrow."

After explaining that I would be going over the handouts several more times before the final product was due, she wanted to know how much of her final grade would be affected by the research paper.

Through this project, I realized that even the best-laid plans need to be adjusted for each student's individual personality style. I also learned just what a nightmare research papers can be.

The different responses and reactions regarding the research paper project can be explained through the ***DISC*** Model of Human Behavior.

Owen, a high "***D***", wants to be in control of this project in terms of the time factor. He does not want this project to linger. He wants it out of the way!

Tamara, a high "***I***", wants to turn this boring project into something fun and adventurous. She wants to have fun and "experience" the research paper.

Autumn, a high "***S***", is relaxed and calm about the entire project. She wants it to be a peaceful experience, and she wants to please the teacher.

Kacy, a high "***C***", wants time to think about her choices. She needs to look at her possible choices from all angles in order to make sure that she is making a wise decision concerning her topic.

Knowing and understanding the principles of ***DISC*** reveal to this teacher that:

"***D***": Likes to do things their way. They are strong-willed and dogmatic. They like to call the shots and tell others what to do.

"***D***": Their motto is "Let's just get it done." Their single-mindedness in reaching a goal leads to the quick accomplishment of the task at hand. They prefer to do things the fastest and most direct way.

"***I***": They believe talking and doing are synonymous. In their quest for popularity and prestige, they are very talkative, but they have short attention spans. They need to get organized and improve their follow-through efforts.

"***I***": Their motto is "Let's do it the fun way." They seek stimulation and variation from the routine. Avoid giving them long-term or repetitive tasks. They like to work in groups.

"***S***": They are seldom in a hurry to complete a task. They want to work at a steady pace. Their cry is, "Give me time!"

"***S***": Their motto is "Let's do it the easy way." They like to utilize shortcuts. They want to avoid unnecessary steps in a process. They enjoy working together as a team.

"***C***": They are calculating, logical and methodical. "**C**s" are very exacting and orderly in their pursuits.

"***C***": Their motto is "Let's do it the right way." They are often overly attentive to details, and they seek to avoid making mistakes. Allow them to find their correct way of accomplishing tasks.

Task: Research papers

DISC Plan:

Allow "***D***" students to turn sections in early.

Give opportunities for the "***I***" students to share some of their information orally or visually with charts, pictures or drawings. Allow "***I***" students opportunities to broaden the research perspectives. They know many people, so let them help in scheduling field trips, in contacting special guest speakers and in contacting the media for publicity.

Give "***S***" students a narrowed down list of suggested topics and work with them to choose a topic suitable to their interests.

Give "***C***" students a detailed handout of directions and requirements. Also give them a checklist with the dates of completion for each requirement.

Art in the Making

Students in my eighth grade class were asked to select a subject and an art medium, and then to design a picture for the spring art contest. After the rules and requirements for completion of the project were explained, I sat back and watched how each student approached his project.

Darnell, my "***D***" student, knew exactly what he wanted to do. He selected his supplies and got to work. He finished his project quickly, so he helped Susan, my "***S***" student, since she had expressed some difficulty with getting started.

India, my "***I***" student, had a brilliant idea about her picture, but before she could finish, she was off visiting everyone in the room. She wanted to know what everyone else had chosen to do. Then she saw her best friend walking down the hall. She could not resist the urge to stick her head out the door and strike up a conversation about her Friday night plans. When she finally got back to her picture, she asked me why I didn't serve them refreshments while they worked!

As mentioned earlier, Susan, an "***S***", had trouble getting started, so she got help from Darnell. She could not decide if she should draw a house with flowers or an entire landscape. Then Susan could not decide whether she should do it in charcoal or watercolors. I saw her eyes well up with tears when Darnell told her to just make up her mind and get to work.

Carla a "***C***", planned her project step-by-step. First, she made sure that all of her supplies were within arm's reach. Next, she designed her drawing area to make sure that what she planned to draw would fit in that space. Then, she asked me if it would be okay to sketch the picture first on another sheet of paper before actually doing the final drawing. While in the middle of sketching, Carla made a mistake, tore the paper into pieces and started all over again.

It was interesting to see all of the different styles and approaches the students were using to create their projects. It was also very helpful to me, as the teacher, to realize each student's personality style would be utilized, not only on this art project, but in every area of his academic life. All of the final projects were unique and special, and so were the artists.

The ***DISC*** Model of Human Behavior was thoroughly demonstrated by these art students.

Darnell, the "***D***" student, was quick to choose his project and get to work. He did not waste one minute. He wanted to get finished more than he wanted to enjoy his work.

India, the "***I***" student, was quick to get to work but was easily distracted. Her socializing and need for fun got in the way of her academic progress.

Susan, the "***S***" student, could not decide what to draw. She received help from Darnell, but his impatience and harsh tone hurt Susan's feelings. That really helped me to see the value in understanding personality styles. Although Darnell's motives were 100% pure and good, he actually hindered Susan's ability by trying to get her to do things using his style instead of her own. Unfortunately, teachers and parents often make this mistake.

Carla, the "***C***" student, was calculating. She planned ahead and arranged her materials before she began. However, when she made a mistake, rather than erasing or being flexible, she started the entire process all over again.

Knowing and understanding the principles of ***DISC*** reveal to this teacher that:

"***D***": Darnell is results-oriented. The "***D***" student sees the end result from the beginning. The "***D***" style loves plans, processes and projects. They are driving and determined. They measure their personal value by their track record and progress. "***D***s" tend to be more concerned over the possibility of losing rather than the prospect of winning.

"***D***": Darnell is quick to finish his project. "***D***" students are very ambitious, productive and energetic. They like to work at a fast pace. Let them take the lead, but be sure to give them guidelines.

"***I***": India's attention span is short and sporadic. "***I***" students tend to be unfocused. They become restless and are easily bored. Inattention to details and low follow-through effort are other shortcomings. They thrive on spontaneity.

"***I***": India immediately gets to work, but she has difficulty midway through the project. "***I***" students are great starters but poor finishers. As Dr. Rohm says, "The "***I***" types need to learn the motto, 'Inch by inch anything is a cinch, but by the yard everything is hard.'" Help your "***I***" type students understand that they aren't bad people for losing interest in a project, but projects still need to be completed. This helps to build personal responsibility into their character. They need short-term projects and frequent breaks to vary the routine. Don't burden them with too many details.

"***S***": Susan has a difficult time beginning her project. "***S***" students are poor starters, but they are great finishers. They are steady, stable and sincere. They like doing things the traditional way.

"***S***": David's frustration and blunt comments hurt Susan's feelings. "***S***" students are usually softhearted. They are sensitive and make loyal and faithful friends. In their desire to be accommodating, they may face the danger of becoming sensitive suckers.

"***C***": Carla's preplanning helped her to make progress on the project. "**C**s" thrive on organization. They are extremely conscientious and highly organized. Disorganization drives them crazy.

"***C***": Carla became too intent on perfection, and this hindered her progress. "***C***" students tend to be precise and detailed. They have an innate need to be right and will drive you crazy with questions. They need to be careful that their perfection doesn't lapse into being too critical.

Task: Art projects

DISC Plan:

Allow "***D***" students to work as artists' aides after completing their own projects.

Allow "***I***" students to socialize while working. Praise and encourage consistency and completion to keep them on track.

Allow "***S***" students to brainstorm with artists' aides to make decisions about their work and to maintain a steady pace.

Allow "***C***" students time to get started, and use continued reassurance and sincere praise. Utilize flexibility in order to help them to finish.

Pop Quiz

Somewhere around midterm, I decided my ninth grade algebra class could use an additional grade. A few of my students had struggled on some of the previous tests, so I felt like a pop quiz on some material that we had recently covered several days in a row would be just the boost that their grades needed.

Laying my trap carefully, I put five simple problems on the board and waited for the bell. They were accustomed to seeing work on the board. Therefore, they would not know it was a pop quiz, until I told them.

When they were all quietly seated, I announced, "Please take out a sheet of paper, and put your name on it..." Before I could finish, Shaw, my high "***C***" student, asked, "Is this a test? Today is Wednesday and math tests can only be given on Mondays and Fridays. So, if it is a math test, then you are in violation of the school's rule." I assured Shaw that it was only a quiz, and that it was perfectly legal.

"This is going to be a piece of cake," bragged Chris, my high "***D***" student. "Anyone care to place a little wager on his score?"

Before I could respond, Will, my "***S***" student, asked, "Would you like for us to circle our answers? Would that make it easier for you to grade?"

During all of this, Bob, the algebra class high "***I***", was waving his hand and fidgeting in his desk. "What is it, Bob?" I asked.

"Have you ever dipped snuff?" Bob asked in a serious tone.

"No, Bob," I said. "But thank you for asking."

The class took the short quiz and turned in their papers. At the end of the period, I returned their graded papers.

Chris said, "I think you made a mistake in grading my

paper. My paper has a 60 on it."

Ever the dry wit, Shaw chirped in, "Wow, you must have cheated!"

Chris retorted, "How would you like a fat lip, man?"

Will, sitting between them, broke out in a cold sweat. "C'mon guys, a 60 isn't so bad."

Shaw, curious to the point of being nosy, looked at Bob and asked, "Bob, what did you make on the quiz?"

As usual, Bob was not paying much attention. His totally unrelated "space cadet" reply was, "I'm not chewing anything. Honest!"

The ***DISC*** Model of Human Behavior is clearly seen in action with the students' different responses to the pop quiz.

Chris, a high "***D***", not only is confident about his performance on the quiz, he even wants to turn it into a competitive event.

Bob, the high "***I***" in the class, has not really been paying much attention to the quiz discussion at all. He appears to be in his own space cadet world.

Will, the "***S***" student, is looking for a way to help the teacher make the grading process easier and to keep peace in the classroom.

Shaw, the "***C***" in the class, questions the test date. He wants to make sure that no rule is being violated. He loves procedure.

Knowing and understanding the principles of ***DISC*** reveal to the teacher that:

"***D***" students are self-assured. These students are very independent and confident. They have a tendency to be prideful and cocky. They thrive on adventurous challenges.

"***D***" students like competition. "***D***s" are enthusiastic and courageous challengers. They love to fight and play to win. They would rather make excuses than point the finger of blame at others.

"***I***" students are interested in people and the activities of people. Relationships are the heartbeat of their existence. They like to be personable and on the go.

"***I***" students tend to be daydreamers with short attention spans. These students are optimistic and hopeful in their thoughts.

"***S***" students like to serve others. They are natural-born social workers who flourish when helping people. These students demontrate care and concern for others.

"***S***" students like to feel that they have made a contribution. They like to support and help. "**S**s" enjoy feeling valued and appreciated. They also work well cooperatively.

"**C**" students want compliance. They abide by the rules and dislike impropriety.

"**C**" students are cautious and thorough. They check it out completely, so that they can be correct.

Task: Math Extra Credit

DISC Plan:

Offer competitive activities for "***D***" students. They love competition and challenges.

Offer interactive puzzles or games for "***I***" students. Talking with others and exchanging ideas excites them.

Offer team activities and team problem solving activities in which "***S***" students may participate. They are dependable and steady teammates and work well in structured situations with defined parameters.

Offer opportunities to teach the material to the rest of the class, or explain the steps of solving a problem for "**C**" students. These students are very wise and gifted, and they need to learn to share their brilliant insights with others.

Historical Differences

Every year my tenth grade world history class is required to complete a major project. The students are given a list of choices from which to choose. Each topic on the list has the same requirements. Students are assigned to teams, and each team has to build one of the suggested structures from the list. When completed, one or all of the team members are required to present an oral report.

One year, one of the groups was especially interesting because of the personality differences. This group included Tyler, the "***D***", Anthony, the "***I***", Lisa, the "***S***" and Amy, the "***C***". As the groups started planning, I heard Tyler say, "All right, let's go for the gold. We can have the most awesome project of all!"

The next remark came from Anthony. "I can do the oral presentation, but you know I'm a busy guy. I have football practice every day after school, and I'm going hunting next week, and I have a girlfriend. So, I'll need plenty of time to prepare for a good presentation."

While Anthony was talking, Lisa sat very quietly. I could tell that she was relieved to know that she would not have to speak in front of the class.

Finally, Amy responded, "Now let's see what all has to be done." She made a list of supplies for the group, divided the items among the members and gave them all a deadline for bringing their items to class.

As the days went by, I noticed that Tyler led the group to select a replica of St. Basil's in Moscow as the topic. Then he dictated how the project was to be completed and worked on the construction. Anthony prepared an excellent oral report and even practiced the presentation with a Russian accent. Lisa did a beautiful job with the artwork, and she supplied refreshments and encouragement daily. Amy handled the details of the project, and she made sure the group was ready to do the presentation.

Needless to say, this group did indeed go for the gold, and the result was an awesome project. Properly utilizing the personality differences resulted in a magnificient presentation.

The ***DISC*** Model of Human Behavior is modeled with this group's personalities:

"***D***": Tyler is a go-getter. He is ready to get busy and is optimistic about the end result.

"***I***": Anthony knows his strength is in presenting material and dealing with people. His busy schedule reveals his love for activity and involvement.

"***S***": Lisa is patient and pleasant. Without understanding personality styles, one would never understand why deep down she is a bit timid and intimidated.

"***C***": Amy likes to be the recorder. She likes to do the planning, and she likes to keep track of the details.

Knowing and understanding the principles of ***DISC*** reveal to the teacher that:

"***D***" students are natural-born leaders. They like directing and orchestrating projects, and they like to delegate.

"***D***" students are doers rather than talkers. They are focused on getting the task done, rather than standing around talking about it. The danger may come in their zeal to do rather than explain or listen.

"***I***" students are excellent communicators. These students are very interactive, and they can talk your ear off. The danger is that they are prone to exaggerate.

"***I***" students love to be around people. "***I***s" are very sociable and personable. They love exposure to people. The danger for them is that they are gullible and easily manipulated.

"***S***" students are good listeners. Patience, approachableness and caring are natural personality traits. They love to get feedback. The danger for this personality style is that they may listen too much and become uncommunicative.

"***S***" students tend to be submissive. These types of students are flexible and cooperative. They are very vulnerable to peer pressure and group consensus.

"***C***" students are very conscientious, and they love details. They are discerning and contemplative, and they check and re-check details. The danger is that they may get lost in the details, rather than seeing the big picture.

"***C***" students are orderly and neat. These types of students are so exacting that they proofread Xerox copies!

Task: Group Presentations

DISC Plan:

Allow "***D***" students to be captains of the group, but teach them to begin to control themselves before trying to control others.

Allow "***I***" students to be the lead presenters, but teach them to share the limelight with others. Also, help them to learn to listen.

Allow "***S***" students to provide support to the group, but teach them to be assertive and show determination.

Allow "***C***" students to be thorough and analytical with details, but teach them to take more risks with a positive attitude.

The Presidential Election

Each year, the first unit which I cover with my seniors in government class includes the concepts of voting, political parties and elections. A mock election is incorporated into this unit. The two purposes of this are for hands-on experience and also to elect a new student council president. I never tire of this unit as I know it will always bring about interesting insights for all of us.

I began this particular unit in the usual way. I split the class into two political parties, and each section created a party name. Then, each section nominated and selected their candidates for the offices of president and vice president.

Darren was the presidential candidate for The Barron Party, and Allie was the presidential candidate for The Free Party. As in the past years, both candidates were high "***I***" personality types. To make matters even more interesting, I agreed to allow John, a high "***D***" personality, to create a third party when he came to me voicing displeasure with his party.

After we established our parties, the next step was to establish the roles that each person would play within their parties during the actual campaign. The Barron Party chose Melissa, a high "***C***", as their campaign manager. The Free Party chose Patrick, also a high "***C***", as their campaign manager. John quickly named himself campaign manager, as well as presidential candidate of his independent party.

Throughout the week, the parties were busy with their campaigns. All party members gracefully agreed to most things established by their respective parties and simply followed the party platform. The "***I***" party members had fun thinking up campaign slogans and talking to people. The "***C***" party members were busy putting everything in exact order, and the "***D***" party members pulled everything together and made it all happen.

The Friday before the Election Day, we held a political forum to debate the issues that were included in the party platforms. Bradley, a high "***D***", was the master of ceremonies, and he followed the agenda created by Kelley, a high "***C***".

Darren and Allie, opposing presidential candidates, each had eight minutes to speak to the student body. These two "***I***" candidates had loads of fun. They told funny jokes and had the entire student body laughing. John, the "***D***" candidate, delivered his eight-minute speech in a matter-of-fact business-like manner. I thought that I was listening to Ross Perot!

Election Day finally came. Precincts had been set, ballots created and the "***S***" personalities, led by Sylvia, served as pollsters. (Even though it made them feel a little uncomfortable, they just couldn't say *no*.) The final ballots were tallied, and it was a close race between all of the candidates. In the end, Allie, the highest "***I***" of them all, won.

John, the "***D***", didn't win, but quickly informed the victor that he was going to be her top advisor!

This mock election gave the teacher great insight into all his students, as well as the workings of ***DISC***.

John, the high "***D***", dared to be different. His independent nature and desire for control led him to create a third party.

Allie and Darren, the high "***I***" types, were popular and known for their fun, social ways. They were friendly, and their carefree attitudes attracted a lot of support.

Sylvia, the high "***S***", was a "behind the scenes" type person. She was supportive and able to contribute in a way that helped all the parties.

Melissa and Patrick, the high "**C**s", were given the roles that required precision and planning. They focused a lot of energy on getting things done right and in the most efficient manner.

Knowing and understanding the principles of ***DISC*** reveal to this teacher that:

"***D***": John will create his own situations when faced with ones that he does not like. He is demanding. He wants to do things his own way, and he wants to have personal control. He likes to make and interpret his own rules and can become critical when things don't go his way.

"***D***": John needs assistance in learning to be a team player. His sense of self-sufficiency and independence can lead him to be insensitive toward others. He needs to learn to relinquish his leadership at times in order to become part of the team.

"***I***": Darren and Allie excel when given the opportunity to motivate people. Their personalities are magnetic and inspiring. They are able to generate a lot of enthusiasm.

"***I***": Darren and Allie need opportunities to transfer talk into action. They need to learn to focus on function in addition to fun. They can't be all mouth and no move. Help them to avoid procrastination by giving them specific and attainable goals.

"***S***": Sylvia likes to feel that she is valuable and a team player. She is cooperative and compatible. She likes participation.

"***S***": Sylvia's desire to please makes it hard for her to say *no*. Her tendency to be a passive and malleable conformist needs to be balanced by times when she is assertive.

"***C***": Melissa and Patrick prefer working with data and structure. They are meticulously analytical and logical. They tend to be myopic when it comes to a goal.

"***C***": Melissa and Patrick need opportunities to present information that they gathered and analyzed. They enjoy letting their work reveal who they are and not just what they can do. They are quite competent and gifted. They want others to notice their accomplishments and to compliment them.

Task: Mock Presidential Elections

DISC Plan:

Assign the "***D***" students the task of managing the election process. They can be captains of candidates' election teams and oversee each team's efforts.

Assign the "***I***" students to help with publicity and the development of jingles, slogans and posters.

Assign the "***S***" students to teams responsible for assisting all the candidates with their multitudinous needs for the campaign.

Assign the "***C***" students to the committee that develops and oversees the rules and regulations of the election. They can lead assigned election committees in their oversight responsibilities, and they can do the tallying of ballot results.

Vive la Difference!

Learning new material can be intimidating to some students, while others thrive on the challenge. These differences in students' personalities and learning styles are vividly clear in high school language classes. My first year teaching French provided excellent examples of the differences in personalities and learning styles.

For two weeks, Monsieur "***C***" asked the same question of me daily. "Why do we have to take a foreign language to graduate? It doesn't make any sense. No one in my family has ever met a French speaking person, and I don't plan on ever going to France."

Monsieur "***I***" always had the best reply. "Chill out, dude. French is the language of love. How do you say 'I love you'? How do you say 'I want a date with you'?"

As I wrote "Je t'aime" and "J'ai rendez-vous avec toi" on the board, the "***I***" students scrambled for pencils and paper. I watched as they carefully wrote down the words.

Meanwhile Monsieur "***C***" had more questions. "Why do the nouns have masculine (le) and feminine (la) articles in front of them? Did they make their language confusing on purpose?" I patiently and thoroughly answered all the questions, and eventually Monsieur "***C***" was convinced that no major conspiracy existed.

Once we were all comfortable with the French mind-set, I gave a project assignment. Each student was to research, then creatively present, some aspect of French life and culture.

Mademoiselle "***D***" presented a poster that concisely summarized the French fashion trends over the past one hundred years. She eagerly wanted to be the first to present her poster. She did an excellent job.

Monsieur "***I***" baked a quiche and a mousse, and he brought chicory coffee for his Real French party. He was the perfect host.

Mademoiselle "***S***" read a poem that she had written entitled "The French." In it, she revealed a great deal about the reasons for certain French customs and habits. She had high praise for everyone's projects, and her support and excitement were deeply appreciated by all.

Mademoiselle "***C***" brought beignets, a type of French pastry, cut in exact-sized rectangles. She had carefully cooked them one at a time to perfection in an electric skillet, just like the French do. She provided us with all of the informative facts about beignets.

We had such a great time presenting the projects that Monsieur "***I***" suggested that we do it once a month. Thus, French Friday was born.

We all look forward to that Friday once a month when we not only share all of the different aspects of French life and culture, but we also share our own differences, as well. As the French would say, "Vive la Difference!"

The ***DISC*** Model of Human Behavior is clearly evident in this classroom.

When given a project assignment with very few guidelines, Mademoiselle "***D***" presented concrete and concise facts regarding French fashion over the past one hundred years. High "***D***s" like to be direct and to the point.

Monsieur "***I***" not only taught the class about French culture and life, but he also turned it into a party where he played the host. High "***I***s" do best in activities where they are entertaining others.

Mademoiselle "***S***" felt secure and comfortable in the class. She felt safe enough to write a poem and express herself. She helped others by encouraging them and praising them. The high "***S***" personality likes a secure and supportive environment.

Mademoiselle "***C***" made it a point to prepare the traditional French beignets exactly as the French do. Then she insisted on discussing the facts surrounding the origin and preparation of the food. The high "***C***" personality insists on discussing the facts.

Knowing and understanding the principles of ***DISC*** reveal to this teacher that:

"***D***"students like the practical and logical approach. They are realistic and practical in implementing tasks and projects.

"***D***" students like bottom line facts. They are direct and to the point. They want to know what will work effectively. They dislike talkers who don't produce.

"***I***" students can turn even mundane activities into fun. Their playful nature wants everything to be entertaining and interesting. As the song says, they "just wanna have fun."

"***I***" students work best in a social environment with social activities. Interaction with others is important to them.

"***S***" students will stick with proven methods because of their need for security and a desire to minimize risks. They dislike instability and sudden changes.

"***S***" students will strive to support and appreciate others as valued members of the team. They are a sentimental stabilizing force.

"***C***" students have high personal standards for themselves due to their intense perfectionism. They can be quite idealistic. Sometimes they are impractical and impossible to satisfy. They prefer to do tasks by themselves in order to do them correctly.

"***C***" students are meticulous in dealing with facts and details. Their orderly research and precision can border on compulsiveness if they aren't careful.

Task: Independent projects/presentations
DISC Plan:

Encourage "***D***" students to develop a project/presentation that also includes a competitive game which all of the students can play.

Encourage "***I***" students to plan a short-term project that can be completed in a few steps. Provide enough break times to vary their schedule.

Encourage "***S***" students to add variety and creativity to their tried and true methods.

Encourage "**C**" students to combine facts with imagination for a well-rounded presentation.

A Big Production

As the choral director, it is my responsibility to present three productions throughout the year. One such production is the senior play. It has been a tradition at the school that the seniors always produce a play, and that play is always a musical. In the past, the production has always had parts for everyone in the senior class in order for each student to get to participate. Some parts are small; some are large. However, traditionally, everyone had a part in the play.

This particular year, a young man, not affiliated with our school in any way, was asked to direct. He was very active in the local theater productions in our town. Stephanie, the president of the senior class and a high "***D***" type personality, told him to choose the play that he thought would be the best one to do, and then to proceed with it.

I helped him with the tryouts. It did not take long for me to realize that there were only twelve available parts in this play, and that there were fifty students in the graduating class. Needless to say, when the cast list was posted, pandemonium broke loose.

One of the students, a very high "**C**" type personality, starting asking, "Who picked that man? Why didn't he choose a play that had fifty parts instead of twelve? This is the most ridiculous thing that has happened all year!"

Two of the students, both "***I***" girls, were initially excited that they were going to be saloon girls in the play. They were laughing about how they were going to be able to dance the Can-Can. However, the more they listened to the other students complain, the angrier these two girls became, because they were not going to be able to sing. After all, that was what they had really wanted to do. Their happiness soon turned to gloom, and I watched them leave with long faces.

The president of the senior class, a "***D***", was furious. I could easily tell that she was upset. I was afraid that she was being too hard on herself for choosing this man as the director. I put my arm around her shoulder and told her not to be too hard on herself. I told her that her intentions were good, and that we all make choices that sometimes are less than perfect. She whirled around and looked at me with total shock. "I'm not upset with myself," she said. "I'm upset with him. I found him, and I gave him a job. Then he did not even choose me for a part. That is so not fair!"

In the midst of all this chaos, the girl who had been cast in the lead role, Mary, a high "***S***" type personality, started crying. She felt as if it was all her fault. She said that she should have never been given the lead, and that she was the reason why her friends were so unhappy. She announced, amid her tears, that she was going to drop out of the play.

It took quite a bit of explaining, and a whole lot of understanding and flexibility, but the show did go on, and we were all the wiser for it.

The ***DISC*** Model of Human Behavior is well demonstrated by this story.

The "***D***" personality style is one that is quick to take control and make a decision. When things do not work out as expected, the "***D***" will probably demonstrate anger.

The "***I***" personality style has a desire to please and maintain relationships at any cost.

It is easy for "***S***s" to accept blame and responsibility for situations that are not actually their fault. They often sacrifice things in order to try and regain peace and harmony.

The "***C***" personality style is always looking at things and situations through logical eyes. When things do not make sense to a "***C***" personality type, he will become critical and sometimes blunt.

Knowing and understanding the principles of ***DISC*** reveal to the teacher that:

"***D***" students believe that their worth is based on the end results. They want to be noticed and validated by their achievements and their competence.

"***D***" students tend to focus on themselves and their own territory. They can easily fall into egocentric thinking. Their sense of independence can lead to a sense of domination.

"***I***" students are moody and emotionally expressive.

"***I***" students tend to let their emotions guide them. They need to be aware of their personal feelings, and they need to focus on facts in addition to feelings.

"***S***" students often express anger or fear with tears. "***S***s" are the most emotional personality style. They tend to think and react emotionally. They often react indirectly.

"***S***" students are softhearted and sensitive. Their sweet disposition makes them congenial and responsive to the needs of others.

"**C**" students are fact-oriented, and that tends to hinder their social skills. They need to learn to be more demonstrative with their emotions and more caring. If they don't, they may become too rigid or negative in their demands.

"**C**" students tend to become overly critical when things do not go right. Their motto is "Don't just get it done – Do it the right way!" They tend to be confrontational and critical. They enjoy being allowed to check on the progress of others to see that mistakes are avoided, and tasks are done correctly.

Task: Group productions

DISC Plan:

Teach "***D***" students to use past struggles to help them display compassion and understanding in present situations. This way they can learn from their past weaknesses, as well as their past strengths.

Teach "***I***" students to be more firm with themselves in dealing with less than favorable situations. They need to learn how to take an independent stand on an issue, especially when facing peer pressure.

Teach "***S***" students how to be more assertive. If not, they may become too passive and weak-willed.

Teach "***C***" students ways to reduce their complaining by cultivating a positive mental attitude. If "***C***" type students are not happy with certain results, they have a tendency to become negative.

Personality Blends

Understanding your most predominate trait as a "***D***", "***I***", "***S***" or "***C***" is just the beginning of understanding your personality. It cannot be stressed enough that no one fits neatly and nicely into just one personality style. Your most predominate trait is most definitely not your only trait!

You also have some aspects of the other traits, as well. We are each a ***blend*** of all four behavior traits to a greater or lesser degree. These different traits work together to create our own unique personalities.

A "***D***" personality can also have some fairly strong "***I***", "***S***" or "***C***" traits. An "***I***" can have some fairly strong "***D***", "***S***" or "***C***" traits. "***S***s" and "***C***s" can also share strengths and/or weaknesses from other types as well.

In each behavioral style, the secondary traits serve our primary trait. While we all possess one trait that can be described as the primary or most predominate one, our secondary traits serve and support our primary trait.

Our goal in understanding our blended style of behavior is to look at our strengths and weaknesses and then make adjustments accordingly. The advantage in understanding our blends is that we can borrow more efficiently from our secondary traits and learn to raise or lower our "***D***", "***I***", "***S***" or "***C***" traits at appropriate times.

Knowing our blended styles and understanding how blends work helps us to understand others and ourselves better. With blends we can grow, learn and develop new ways of becoming all that we were meant to be.

The following four scenarios will reveal how understanding a

Personality Blend can help you build better relationships or create more effective teams.

As you have read through this material, you have probably found yourself thinking, "I feel a lot like this one personality style, but I also feel like I have some of the other styles in me, too." You do – it should be obvious that no one is purely a "***D***", "***I***", "***S***" or "***C***". No one will fit neatly and nicely into just one personality style.

You will always find yourself identifying with some of the behaviors and preferences of other personality types. For survival, you have learned to accommodate your own style to a variety of different situations.

However, this experience of adjusting yourself to your situation has probably made it difficult for you to identify and separate your acquired, or environmental, traits from your natural, or genetic, traits. So, how can you identify your most dominant personality style? You can begin by seeking to understand what drives you – that is, what your passion is, rather than just what you are doing each day to get by.

At times, circumstances force you to use a particular style with which you are very uncomfortable, but adapting yourself to these circumstances will also cause you to grow in new areas. Remember, you are not completely lacking in the personality skills of any of your own, less dominant "***D***", "***I***", "***S***" or "***C***" areas!

The chart on the following page shows how each style is "connected" to the styles adjacent to it. This indicates that your own particular style "bleeds over" into, or borrows from, other personality types. "Borrowing" from your other, less dominant traits is part of fitting in and working with others.

You may have noticed, from your own experience, that the style which is diagonally opposite your primary style ("***D***" and "***S***" are opposites, as are "***I***" and "***C***") is the one you struggle with most and understand least. Although it may be unfamiliar to you, you can learn to employ it – and in some cases, you already have! This, by the way, is good news! We can grow, learn and develop new ways of becoming all that we were meant to be!

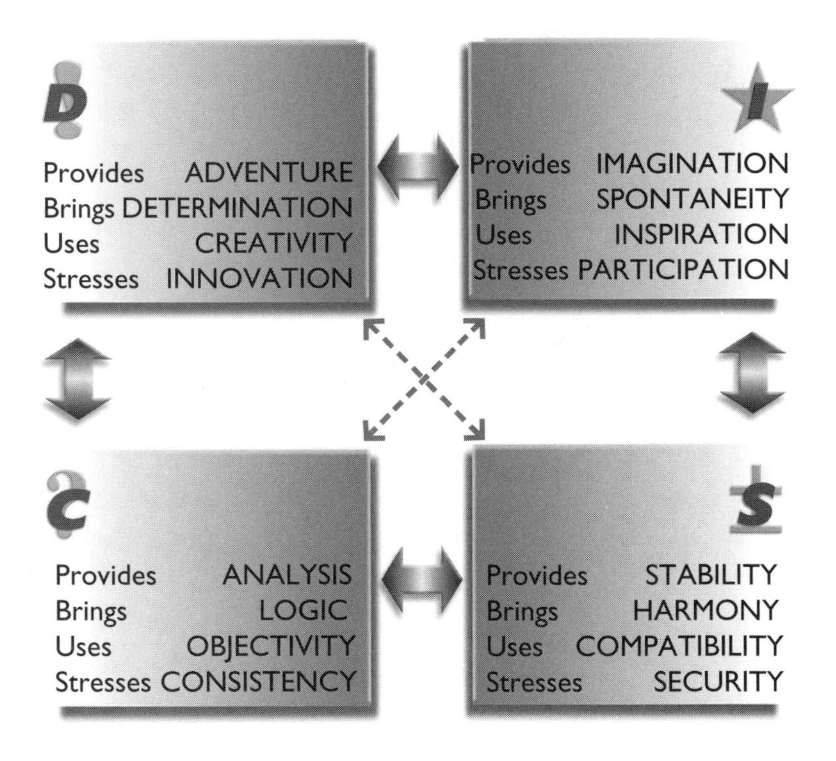

While arrows connect adjacent traits, there are broken arrows connecting "***D***" with "***S***" and "***I***" with "***C***". This is because they are not "naturally" complementary traits. They are usually thought of as contrasting traits. Although these "opposite" skills may be unfamiliar, they still may be developed.

In this section, we will learn about "blends" of personality types – how different traits work in your personality to create your own, unique personality style. We'll see how a "***D***" type person can also have some fairly strong "***I***", "***S***" or "***C***" qualities. An "***I***" can have fairly strong "***D***", "***S***" or "***C***" traits. "**S**s" and "**C**s" can also share strengths from the other types.

Most commonly, people have one very dominant style, backed up by a secondary style. With such people, two plotting points will be above the midline and two plotting points will fall below the midline. It is also possible for people to have only one very dominant style above the midline, with the other three styles falling below the midline. And some people have three styles above the midline, with only one below the midline. If those variables seem confusing, imagine that each of those styles vary in strength and intensity from person to person. But that's where our differences in personality come from – that's what makes people so fascinating to study. As you look at the charts on the following pages, you can develop a "lab" in your mind – and everywhere you go, you will be able to see people through your "personality lens!"

"Dragnet"

"Dom, de dom, dom; dom, de dom, dom, dummmmmmmmmmmmmmmm." It was Friday morning, April twelfth. The city is Batesville. My partner is Frank Smith. My name is Friday. I'm a cop.

We were working the school division – first grade, little folks. He and I were dispatched by the department to promote the "Clean up - Paint up - Fix up" campaign for the city. We were a good team, and everything was under control.

Danny, a first grader and a "***D/I***" blend, recognized our squad car when we pulled up to the school. His job was to pound erasers on the concrete blocks outside the building. Evidently he did his job well. We noticed layers of slightly damp chalk dust residue from the day before and the day before that.

Danny proudly took charge. He escorted us quickly into the building, flung open the door to his classroom and, with little regard for the teacher, bellowed, "They're here! I saw them while I was cleaning the erasers."

The teacher thanked Danny for his help and asked the other children to put away their books and take a seat on the floor. Danny promptly began instructing the children where to put their books and where to sit on the floor. "Come on. We don't have all day," Danny said loudly to the class. I could tell he was losing patience with the slower moving students. After the students were seated, Danny looked at his classmates sitting on the floor and said, "Sit in a circle. That way, you can see better." Quickly the children complied.

I began to speak to the class, "Boys and girls, our mascot's name is Woodsy Owl. Frank and I are here today to ask for your help. We..."

Danny shot up from the floor and exclaimed, "You can count on me. I am a good helper. I clean the erasers every day and..."

The teacher interrupted Danny by saying, "Thank you, Danny. Now please sit down and let them finish." I could tell Danny was energetic, to say the least.

I continued to explain that we wanted all the children not to litter our beautiful city. We had banners, posters and balloons for the children. As we passed them out, Danny was beside himself. He was talking with his classmates and clapping his hands with glee over the goody bags we had for them.

Once the class settled down, I told them that we wanted them to talk to others and encourage them to keep our city beautiful. "I know you all are just beginning to read, but would someone care to read Woodsy Owl's slogan for us?"

Of course, again Danny shot up like a rocket with his hand waving in the air. Since no one else seemed to want to tackle the task, I looked at Danny and nodded for him to begin reading. Danny looked intently at the slogan which read "Give a Hoot, Don't Pollute!" For a minute, he tried to sound out the words. I could see by the puzzled look on his face that he was concentrating intensely. Then, just when I was about to offer my help, a proud smile came to Danny's face as he exclaimed loudly, "Give a hoot, Don't Poot!"

The story you have heard is true. The names have been changed to protect the innocent.

The blended style of the "***D/I***" in the ***DISC*** Model of Human Behavior is evident with the illustration of Danny.

Danny is outgoing in his blended behavioral style. He takes the initiative to show the guests to the classroom and also takes control when the class needs to be organized.

Danny also tends to be fast paced. His internal motor is always running at a high speed. He is enthusiastic, positive and very confident. In fact, sometimes he has more confidence than he has ability!

Knowing and understanding the blended style of the "***D/I***" personality will reveal to the teacher that:

Those with the "***D/I***" blend have a difficult time understanding situations until they have experienced them.

Those with the "***D/I***" blend have confident and bold attitudes.

Those with the "***D/I***" blend work in bursts of energy. They do much better on short-term projects.

Those with the "***D/I***" blend are high on enthusiasm and low on patience.

Those with the "***D/I***" blend like variety and action.

Strategies for working with the "*D/I*" blend:

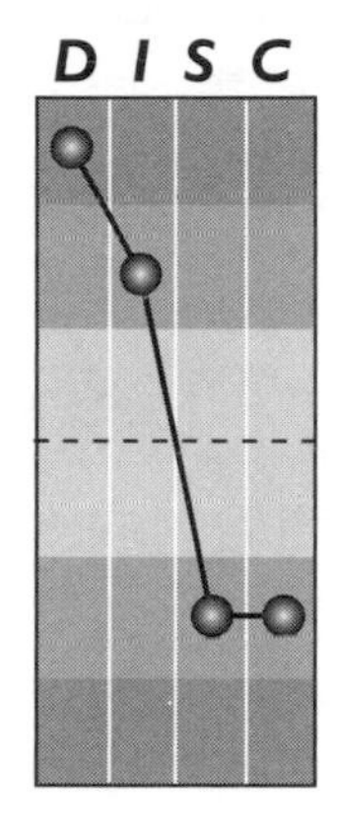

When giving an assignment, provide structure but add variety and opportunities for action. Keep statements and instructions simple and straightforward.

Help the "***D/I***" student to think before acting.

Help the "***D/I***" student to stay on task by showing interest and offering praise.

Give "***D/I***" students opportunities to look for innovative solutions and new possibilities.

Knowing and understanding the blended style of the "***D/I***" personality will reveal to the teacher that:

1. Those with the blend have a difficult time understanding situations until they have experienced them. They need to put into practice what they have learned in order to apply their gained insights. They have assertive convictions. "***D/I***" students need to concentrate less on speaking and more on listening to the opinions, experiences and insights of others so that they can learn to appreciate them. They enjoy being active and having direct, participatory and firsthand experiences instead of imaginary or vicarious assignments. In other words, they enjoy doing something, rather than merely reading about something or being told about it.

2. Those with the "***D/I***" blend have confident and bold attitudes. These students are self-confident and courageous, and they are self-starters. They like to express their strong egos and are not afraid to take risks. They like to think about the future and all of its possibilities.

3. Those with the "***D/I***" blend work in bursts of energy. They do much better on short-term projects. "***D/I***" students don't like to be overloaded with excessive details. They do, however, need concise, clearly defined goals and conclusions with specific time frames in their assignments. Their energy and enthusiasm fuel their shorter attention spans. In addition, they like having their work checked immediately upon completion.

4. Those with the "***D/I***" blend are high on enthusiasm and low on patience. They dislike sitting still and listening for long periods of time. Rather, they like studying about things which have immediate, quickly attainable and practical goals, values, or usages. Upon their completion of the task, be sure to make specific comments on their work, rather than just giving them check marks or colorful stickers.

5. Those with the "***D/I***" blend like variety and action. They dislike repetition. The same old routine is boring to them. Instead, they like stimulation, change and new ideas. Allow them the opportunity to make personal choices within specified boundaries, and then step aside and let them go. However, a word of warning: "***D/I***" students like to begin a project, but they leave the completion of the project to others.

More strategies for working with the "*D/I*" blend:

1. When giving an assignment, provide structure but add variety and opportunities for action. "***D/I***" students like challenging workloads which keep them stimulated and interested. They also like opportunities for advancement, such as being the class monitor, teacher's assistant, teaching or leading the class.

2. Keep statements and instructions simple and straightforward. They like completing assignments or procedures one step at a time. "***D/I***" students learn well in an organized, task-oriented environment.

3. Help the "***D/I***" student to think before acting. They need to think out loud with other students giving them feedback. They like to be asked questions which have specific correct answers, rather than open-ended questions which require speculation or opinions.

4. Help the "***D/I***" students to stay on task by showing interest and offering praise. "***D/I***" students have super egos and like to feel admired and important. They thrive on recognition and awards as incentives. They need to be thanked and rewarded for their contributions. They are motivated by praise. Be sure to give them your time and attention, as well as giving them positive feedback for their progress and accomplishments.

5. Give "***D/I***" students opportunities to look for innovative solutions and new possibilities. "***D/I***" students are inquisitive and creative problem solvers. They like innovation. They prefer to have opportunities to transfer ideas into action through creative exploration and positive manipulation. They like to see immediate and tangible results from their efforts.

Vera

As the librarian of a school, I get the privilege of meeting all of the children and reading to them once a week. There is something magical about watching children huddled in a circle, listening wide-eyed as you read them a story. They are so lovable at that time. On this particular day, however, one student stole my heart forever.

Vera was a vivacious fourth grader and an "***I/S***" blend. She would come to school wearing earrings and lipstick. She was at school for one reason and one reason only: to have fun. She would sit and hold hands with her friends, and she would talk and make funny faces when I read aloud. It was hard to compete with Vera.

On this Wednesday afternoon, I was reading a story entitled *No Jumping on the Bed!* It is a delightful story with hilarious illustrations. It is about a little boy whose father scolded him each night at bedtime for jumping on the bed. His father warned him that if he kept jumping on the bed, he would fall through the floor, and that is exactly what happened.

As I was reading this story, I noticed Susan had covered her mouth with her hands. At first, I thought Susan had covered her mouth to keep from laughing at the story. However, as the tale unfolded, Susan's face began to turn a peculiar shade of green.

In the book, a boy and his bed fall down through the bedroom floor of the apartment and land on Miss Hattie's dining room table where she is eating a huge plate of spaghetti and meatballs. Who knows whether it was the sight of all that spaghetti swimming all over the page or the mere thought of eating it that did it to poor Susan, but all of a sudden, she removed her hands from her mouth and proceeded to lose her lunch all over the carpet.

The scene that followed was pure pandemonium. Some students jumped up, while some sat stunned amid shouts of "Gross," and "Sick."

James bounded in from one of his frequent bathroom visits and exclaimed, "Cool! I did that once playing T-ball, but mine looked like popcorn, and I DID IT OUTSIDE!"

Poor Susan glanced around the room with an expression of shock. Her lower lip began to quiver, and tears began to run down her cheeks. Before I could gather my wits about me to handle the situation, Vera stood up and walked over to Susan. She took Susan's hands in hers and said, "Don't be embarrassed. You couldn't help it. Come with me. I will help you clean yourself up in the bathroom and then walk you to the office to call your mom." Vera put her arm around Susan, and before she led her out of the library, she turned to the class and said, "Tell Susan that you all hope she feels better." The entire class complied.

My heart swelled with gratitude and pride as I watched Vera walk out the door. She was rubbing Susan's back and telling her that it was going to be okay.

What a day it had been! I believe, with all my heart, that Susan will never forget the day that she got sick in the library. That humiliation is one of a child's worst nightmares. However, I know that Susan will never forget the friend who took her by the hand and led her from one of life's greatest embarrassments into the security of a mother's gentle touch.

The blended style of the "***I/S***" in the ***DISC*** Model of Human Behavior is demonstrated in the story of Vera.

Vera is people-oriented. She loves being with her friends, and no one is a stranger. "***I/S***s" thrive on recognition and approval. They let their emotions guide them.

Vera is thoughtful, empathetic and willing to bend over backward to please others. Vera displays all of these traits in helping Susan. She even uses her influence with the other students to make Susan feel comfortable.

Knowing and understanding the blended style of the "***I/S***" personality will reveal to the teacher that:

Those with the "***I/S***" blend have strong social/ relational abilities.

Those with the "***I/S***" blend desire harmony and are disturbed by conflict.

Those with the "***I/S***" personality blend need to be appreciated and praised.

Those with the "***I/S***" blend like to leave decisions open-ended.

Those with the "***I/S***" blend structure their lives according to their feelings.

Strategies for working with the "*I/S*" blend:

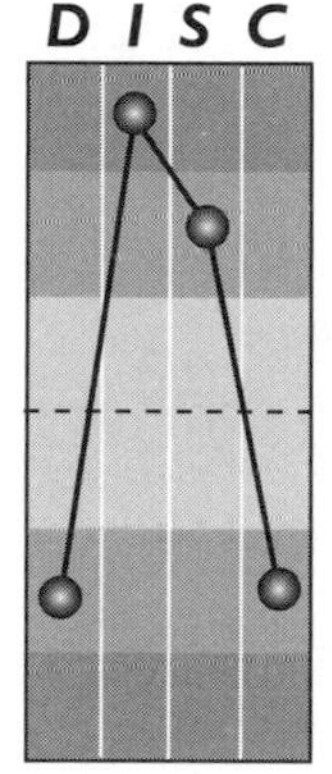

Provide opportunities for interpersonal activities in class.

Provide activities that use imagination and creativity.

Structure lessons so that they are clear, and set limits with specific deadlines.

Encourage progress by giving approval and praise often.

Reprimand the "*I/S*" blend with a gentle hand. This student will not respond well to harsh criticism.

Knowing and understanding the blended style of the "*I/S*" personality will reveal to the teacher that:

1. Those with the "*I/S*" blend have strong social/relational abilities. They like involvement with group experiences and projects in which they have opportunities for sharing personal thoughts, opinions and experiences with other students in the group. While working on a project, they like talking and socializing with a friend or being part of a collaborative team effort. The "*I/S*" student likes to develop ongoing relationships.

2. Those with the "*I/S*" blend desire harmony and are disturbed by conflict. They are mild-mannered students who don't like confrontation. "*I/S*" students avoid arguments and fighting, because it is stressful to them. They prefer non-aggressive environments which are relaxed and comfortable.

3. Those with the "*I/S*" personality blend need to be

appreciated and praised. They need to receive personal attention from the teacher. They also need to feel liked and admired. "***I/S***" students need to be given public credit and recognition, sincere compliments, attention and personal encouragement in order to fully succeed.

4. Those with the "***I/S***" blend like to leave decisions open-ended. They prefer to interact and bounce their ideas and opinions off of other students. They like to share their personal experiences and feelings with others for feedback before they come to their final, but not obligatory, decision.

5. Those with the "***I/S***" blend structure their lives according to their feelings. They think emotionally, and their frame of reference for life is their emotions. In fact, they are quite open to discuss these emotions with others. They prefer activities which help them to learn about themselves and their feelings. They like studying subjects which affect their life experiences rather than studying facts or theories.

More strategies for working with the "*I/S*" blend:

1. Provide opportunities for interpersonal activities in class. They like interactive lessons and activities between the teacher and the student, as well as students working together. They like to be shown what to do by another person rather than non-personalized instructions.

2. Provide activities that use imagination and creativity. "***I/S***" students dislike mere memorization, rote learning and repetition. They like to be stimulated and challenged. They like to personally experience what they are learning.

3. Structure lessons so that they are clear, and set limits with specific deadlines. They need help with getting organized and prioritizing tasks. They need to see the "big picture." "***I/S***" students like working on one thing at a time with tried and proven methodologies which work and produce results. This gives them a sense of achievement and security in the classroom.

4. Encourage progress by giving approval and praise often. "***I/S***" students need personal attention, encouragement and feedback. They thrive on being praised for their good work and accomplishments. This makes them feel important and appreciated.

5. Reprimand the "***I/S***" blend with a gentle hand. This student will not respond well to harsh criticism. "***I/S***" students are sensitive and fearful, and they prefer non-threatening situations. They respond better to a warm, reassuring, affirmative and optimistic approach when dealing with their conduct. Otherwise, they will tend to shut down or disengage from you or the situation.

"S/C" is for Stephen Celt

Every teacher has a student that stands out in his mind and heart more than any other student. Without a doubt, for me, that student would be Stephen Celt.

I taught Stephen in eleventh grade literature. I knew from the beginning that he was a special young man. Stephen had an "***S/C***" personality blend. He was reserved in his manner. He was never one to quickly attack a project or run for class office. However, his strong sense of commitment always impressed me. He impressed the other students too. It did not take the other students in the class long to realize that Stephen was definitely the one that they wanted in their group when it was project time.

All through Stephen's senior year, he continued to stop by my room and talk to me. Other seniors were well into planning their second semester of college while Stephen was still trying to decide what college he wanted to attend. He liked to be systematic and cautious when it came to making decisions.

I looked forward to the visits that Stephen and I would have. It isn't often that a teacher is able to connect with a student, but Stephen and I definitely did. It was exciting to see him grow up.

One day, he asked me what I thought about a particular female friend. When I told him that I thought that she was pretty, he said, "Yes, she is." Then he asked, "What do you think about her on the inside?" That question surprised me a bit. I had been consulted many times about a girl's looks but never about a girl's character. That was Stephen's concern, however. He was incredibly discerning, and he could see through a facade.

Stephen graduated and attended a college in another state.

He wrote to me throughout his first two years of college. He even visited my classroom to see me when he came home for the holidays. However, I transferred schools during Stephen's senior year of college, and we lost touch. I later heard that Stephen had graduated and was attending medical school in another state. That did not surprise me at all, because Stephen was a determined and tenacious young man.

A couple of years ago, I was in a local grocery store, and I heard a deep voice call my name. I turned around, and to my surprise, it was Stephen. We greeted each other, and he told me that he was a pediatrician. He said that he was married, and he and his wife were expecting their first child in two months.

When it came time to say goodbye, Stephen surprised me a bit. He hugged me like a little child and said, "Thank you for understanding me and letting me be me."

Thirty-four years of teaching and every single day was worth it just to hear those ten little words.

The blended style of the "***S/C***" in the ***DISC*** Model of Human Behavior is clearly illustrated in the story of Stephen. His behavioral style is reserved. He is calm and steady and often overlooked, because he is so low key. His classmates, however, realize that Stephen's blended style is the glue that usually holds things together. That is why most students admire his stability.

Stephen tends to be slower paced. His internal motor runs at a consistent, steady speed. He is cautious in his approach to things and is reluctant to make decisions.

Knowing and understanding the blended style of the "***S/C***" personality will reveal to the teacher that:

Those with the "***S/C***" blend have a difficult time experiencing situations until they understand them.

Those with the "***S/C***" blend work steadily and with even-paced energy.

Those with the "***S/C***" blend tend to be high on patience and low on enthusiasm.

Those with the "***S/C***" blend tend to think before acting.

Those with the "***S/C***" blend like to apply personal experience to specific problems.

Those with the "***S/C***" blend enjoy using a wide variety of resources and materials without being burdened by too many routines or procedures.

Strategies for working with the "***S/C***" blend:

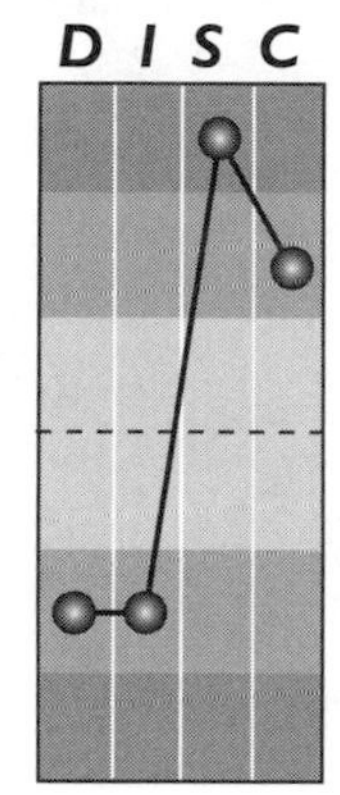

Allow time for this cautious and questioning style.

Keep statements and instructions clear and specific.

Give assignments that require detailed work and critical thinking skills.

Encourage them to share their ideas, and you be willing to share your ideas with them.

Provide a peaceful and quiet area in the classroom for them to concentrate.

Knowing and understanding the blended style of the "***S/C***" personality will reveal to the teacher that:

1. Those with the "***S/C***" blend have a difficult time experiencing situations until they understand them. They need to be allowed enough time so that they can learn by personal discovery and insight rather than by lecture. They need to understand the lessons on a personal level.

2. Those with the "***S/C***" blend work steadily and with even-paced energy. They like to be able to work at their own predictable pace in a stable environment. However, they need to learn to be flexible and adapt to varied situations and timeframes for future "real world" experiences.

3. Those with the "***S/C***" blend tend to be high on patience and low on enthusiasm. "***S/C***" students enjoy opportunities in which they are able to use their imaginations and be creative. They need to learn to be more self-motivated and to speed up their activities when launching new projects.

4. Those with the "***S/C***" blend tend to think before acting. They dislike taking risks and don't like to be rushed or pushed in their activities. They need to plan and think through situations and assignments before they begin tasks. Their thinking is very innovative, and they like to think "outside of the box." They dislike surprises or abrupt changes, and they need time to think about changes and adaptive strategies before the changes occur. You must be patient, but firm, with them.

5. Those with the "***S/C***" blend like to apply personal experience to specific problems. "***S/C***" students are very gifted and insightful. They like drawing on their personal judgments and practical knowledge. The teacher must plan and organize in a creative way for the "***S/C***" students.

6. Those with the "***S/C***" blend enjoy using a wide variety of resources and materials without being burdened by too many routines and procedures. Variety is, indeed, not only the spice of life but also the substance, as well.

More strategies for working with the "*S/C*" blend:

1. Allow time for their cautious and questioning style. "***S/C***" students like dealing with open-ended questions and problem solving activities which require collecting, organizing and evaluating data through both deductive and inductive reasoning. They need to be allowed enough time to thoroughly check things out before arriving at a decision. However, they do need to learn that there are varied, but correct, approaches to tasks and problems.

2. Keep statements and instructions clear and specific. "***S/C***" students like to know what will happen ahead of time and what is expected of them next. They don't like

to be surprised or caught off guard. They like to do tasks which have specific purposes or goals.

3. Give assignments that require detailed work and critical thinking skills. They like a gradual introduction to new material. They are very adept at problem solving activities which require imagination and creativity. However, the teacher must give them adequate time to plan and organize for the assignment.

4. Encourage them to share their ideas, and you be willing to share your ideas with them. "***S/C***" students have valuable insights and expertise which they enjoy sharing with others to help and support them. Allow them plenty of opportunities for their own unique and individual artistic expressions.

5. Provide a peaceful and quiet area in the classroom for them to concentrate. "***S/C***" students are neat and low key. They need an environment which is relaxed, calm, stable, secure, quiet and free of stress, tension or distractions. They like to work on specific tasks at the same time of day and in the same place. Consistency is the key to success with the "***S/C***" student.

Insectlopedia

After my fifth grade class had spent a rather tedious three weeks on an insect unit, I wanted to assign a project that would be both fun and productive. I decided that it would be a good idea for the students to get into groups and create their very own insect. The groups would construct a model of their original insect and present it to the class. We would then have a "boogie bug bash!"

All of the students loved this idea. Actually, all the students loved this idea except Seth. Seth, a "***C/D***" blend, did not want to work in a group. He immediately asked me if he could work alone. All the coaxing in the world would not convince him otherwise. Not wanting to make this a stressful project, I gave in to his pleas and allowed him to work alone.

Seth immediately went to work. He created a checklist of all of the items he needed and a step-by-step "to do" list for his model. He carefully drew diagram after diagram, showing what his model was going to look like. Every day I noticed Seth making progress with his model and checking off the items on his list.

After the third day, I walked by Seth's model and noticed that instead of constructing an original insect, he had built a model of a real insect. "Seth," I said, "your model is a real insect, but the directions were to create your very own insect."

He looked at me for a second, and in a matter-of-fact tone said, "I know, but that is a stupid idea. What good is a make- believe insect? We studied real insects, so my model is going to be a real insect. "With that, he went right back to work. I decided to leave him alone at that moment until I had a chance to think about what I should do.

The next day was presentation day. All of the students were

excited about sharing their creations. As the groups presented their make-believe insects and told about their imaginary abilities, I noticed Seth seething with impatience.

When it came time for Seth to make his presentation, I explained to the students that Seth had decided to construct a model of a real insect. I heard a few sighs, but I was quick to squash those before they grew too loud.

Seth had his model wrapped in a black garbage bag and had not unveiled it to anyone before his presentation. He began his presentation in a business-like manner. He soon had the total attention of everyone in the class. I could not believe it, but I was actually interested in what he was saying. I thought that we had covered all of the information on insects, but I was wrong.

Seth continued discussing the interesting facts about his real insect, and then he removed his model from the garbage bag. It was incredible! For a moment, we thought that we were looking at the real thing! Seth had done a beautiful job constructing his model.

All of the students moved closer to get a better look at it. Seth continued answering questions about the insect and even demonstrated the flight pattern with the model. I sat back, watched in awe and realized that no one, including the teacher, can ever learn enough about insects.

The blended style of the "***C/D***" in the ***DISC*** Model of Human Behavior is illustrated with the story of Seth. Seth is task-oriented in his behavior style. He likes working with facts. He likes to work alone, and he is careful to do things correctly.

Seth likes to plan. He prioritizes and itemizes and constantly keeps track of his progress. Seth enjoys form and function. He thinks there is nothing better than things working the way that they were meant to work.

Knowing and understanding the blended style of the "***C/D***" personality will reveal to the teacher that:

Those with the "***C/D***" blend value logic over emotion.

Those with the "***C/D***" blend often hurt others' feelings without knowing it.

Those with the "***C/D***" blend ignore their feelings and concentrate on facts.

Those with the "***C/D***" blend take pleasure in finishing projects.

Strategies for working with the "*C/D*" blend:

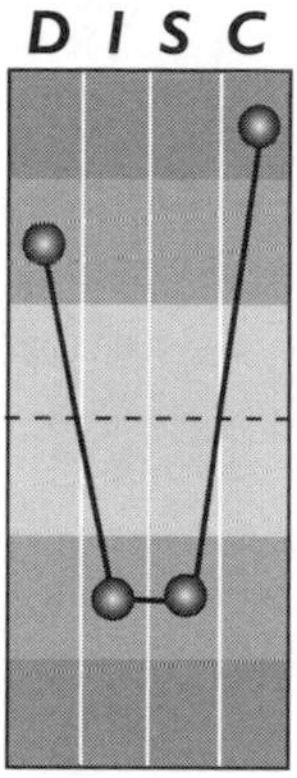

D I S C

Provide opportunities for them to analyze and assimilate facts.

Allow them to be in charge of some administrative duties.

Help them to take others' feelings into consideration.

Provide itemized checklists and "to do" lists with projects.

Give them opportunities to work in groups (in which you closely monitor their interactions) in order to help develop their social skills.

Knowing and understanding the blend style of the "***C/D***" personality will reveal to the teacher that:

1. Those with the "***C/D***" blend value logic over emotion. They are emotionally cool and sometimes aloof. They like to be challenged intellectually and logically. They like to study theoretical, abstract or hypothetical ideas and how things are related. "***C/D***" students are good problem solvers who like to use their brains for discussing or debating a point on the basis of logical analysis. They need to know the WHY, as well as the WHAT, of a situation through deductive reasoning.

2. Those with the "***C/D***" blend often hurt others' feelings without knowing it. They are self-centered and control their own emotions. "***C/D***" students tend to be overly critical and faultfinding. Occasionally, they can be controlling and manipulative, and they need to be on their guard against these tendencies.

3. Those with the "***C/D***" blend ignore their feelings and concentrate on facts. They can be emotionally distant in their even-temperedness. "***C/D***" students have high personal standards and tend to be myopic. They become focused on a goal to the point of the exclusion of their personal feelings. They want to concentrate on having facts make sense to them.

4. Those with the "***C/D***" blend take pleasure in finishing projects. They have great determination and tenacity. They know how to accomplish a task. They enjoy following directions to get a correct conclusion.

5. Those with the "***C/D***" blend like to work independently and to think for themselves. They are self-motivated learners who prefer self-directed activities. "***C/D***" students like to develop their own unique strategies or plans for accomplishing a task. They are good at collecting and evaluating data on their own. They don't like the teacher looking over their shoulder and frequently checking on their progress.

More strategies for working with the "*C/D*" blend:

1. Provide opportunities for them to analyze and assimilate the facts. "***C/D***" students are intuitive and are motivated by self-exploration of materials. They do not like confusion or chaos. They work cautiously, conscientiously and carefully. They like opportunities to put what they have learned to immediate and practical use.

2. Allow them to be in charge of some administrative duties. They are natural-born leaders and administrators. They enjoy

leading others. "***C/D***" students excel at organizing activities or materials.

3. Help them to take others' feelings into consideration. "***C/D***" students can be aggressive, threatening or even revengeful if pushed. They need to learn to be less serious and to tone down their criticism and perfectionistic expectations of others. "***C/D***" types need to work on being friendly and showing appreciation of others.

4. Provide itemized checklists and "to do" lists with projects. "***C/D***" students are orderly, organized and structured. They enjoy working their way step-by-step through lists of specific procedures or materials.

5. Give them opportunities to work in groups (in which you closely monitor their interactions) in order to help develop their social skills. "***C/D***" students naturally prefer to do things by themselves. They need to learn how to work cooperatively and collaboratively, as well as how to delegate responsibilities to others.

6. Provide rational purposes and explanations for activities and projects. They are naturally inquisitive. If you tell them the WHY of a task, "***C/D***" students will characteristically take care of the WHAT and HOW.

Combinations

The most valuable aspect of ***D-I-S-C*** is not in finding out what "type" you are. (Although it is excellent information to possess, it is not the pot of gold at the end of the rainbow.) The greatest value in using the material is learning how to understand others and becoming skilled at adjusting and adapting your own style when you are in their presence. After all, you are the only person that you can really control. This is invaluable information for a teacher.

Don't get me wrong. It is interesting and entertaining to discover who we really are and to learn about other personality types. However, we should not be satisfied with that discovery alone. It is after we learn about our own personality style that the real application begins. If we are wise, we begin the process of working on our personality in order to adjust our behavior to be the best person that we can be. The goal is to make our personality a project, not a topic of conversation.

When my own unique blend of personality traits and your unique blend of personality traits come together, they create a combination. The word ***Combination*** reflects how people relate to each other.

Each of us has a distinctive, individual blend. When a person begins to interact with another person, the two become a combination. As two people work together, they produce a combination that is unique to them.

How we behave around each other, how we react to each other and how we interact with each other are heavily influenced by our own unique blend of traits combined with the traits of another individual. We each bring benefits and pitfalls into every relationship.

Some combinations generally work together harmoniously, while others require more effort, time and understanding. For us to work together and become a winning combination, it will require adjusting and adapting from both sides. In any successful relationship, both individuals will need to adjust their personality styles from time to time.

When we focus on things from our own perspective only, we become one-dimensional. However, as we understand and work with our differences, we can create new dimensions. We can strengthen relationships between teacher and students and improve the chances for meaningful communication and academic success. This concept is what combinations are all about. This concept is ultimately what this entire book is about.

U.F.J.S.

(A "***D***" TYPE TEACHER WORKING WITH ***D-I-S-C*** STUDENTS.)

As a "***D***" type teacher of an eighth grade math class, I like to be in control of the class at all times. So, imagine my dilemma when, in the middle of class, the door to my classroom flew open, and something zoomed through the air and landed in the center of the floor in the front of the room.

I quickly walked over to the object, only to discover that some prankster had thrown a jock strap into my classroom.

Almost immediately, John, a "***D***" student, and I raced to the door and threw the door open. We tried to see if we could get a glimpse of the culprit. The two of us fought for space in the narrow doorway and only succeeded in getting momentarily stuck. John insisted on running down the hall after the person. I said, "No." But he went anyway.

When I turned from the door, I saw Alex, an "***I***" student, holding the jock strap in front of himself, modeling it for the class. As he paraded up and down the rows, I heard him ask, "Does this belong to anyone in here?" The class broke out in laughter, as Alex continued to prance around the room.

Once the laughter subsided, I verbally reprimanded Alex. I told him that if he wanted to be a clown, he should join the circus. But, if he wanted to pass eighth grade math, he should get serious. With that, he threw the jock strap over his shoulder.

The jock strap landed in front of Jason's desk. Jason, an "***S***" student, inconspicuously kicked the strap under his desk and away from Mary Beth's sight. His face was flushed red as he quickly got back to work. I promptly asked him to retrieve the strap from the place where he had kicked it and to bring it to me. He looked as if I had just asked him to model it!

Kevin, the "**C**" student of the class, walked over to the desk, picked the athletic supporter up with his pencil, being careful not to touch it and placed it in a large envelope which he had gotten off my desk. He, then, wrote Unidentified Flying Jock Strap on the front of the envelope and put it on my desk.

Then Kevin asked, "What are you going to do with it?"

I said, "Take it to the office after class, or take it to the lost and found."

He then asked me what I thought that would accomplish. I felt like I was being interrogated! He continued asking me question after question. Then he explained that he thought what we really needed to do was to find the person who threw it into the classroom. He said that the guilty person needed to be suspended. Kevin then gave me the slim statistics on the possibility of finding out the person's identity. A debate ensued, and by now, twenty-five minutes of class time had gone down the drain. I thought to myself, "They didn't teach me how to handle these classroom challenges in my educational courses in college!"

The combination of a "**D**" teacher interacting with each of the personality types is illustrated in this story.

The "**D**" teacher and the "**D**" student had the same goal but struggled over the way to accomplish it.

The "**D**" teacher wanted control, but the "***I***" student wanted to impress others. The "**D**" teacher could not understand why this student was not taking the situation seriously.

The "**D**" teacher intimidated the "***S***" student. Without meaning to, the teacher verbally embarrassed him and belittled him.

The "**D**" teacher and the "**C**" student engaged in a power struggle. The teacher thought that he was right. The "**C**" student thought that he was more right.

STRATEGIES A "*D*" TEACHER SHOULD USE WHEN WORKING WITH *D-I-S-C* STUDENTS:

A "*D*" student must learn to respect and trust his "*D*" teacher, or there will be conflicts. The teacher must earn this trust and respect. Never force issues or give ultimatums to the "*D*" students. Rather, give them options and choices. This will help them feel like they have some control.

An "*I*" student tends to feel that his "*D*" teacher does not care enough about the feelings of students. He feels that the "*D*" teacher is too harsh with everyone. Therefore, it is important to loosen up and relax your control a little bit. Seek to interact and listen to their concerns a little more. Show your feelings with facial expressions along with your words.

An "*S*" student tends to feel secure with a "*D*" teacher, as long as the teacher demonstrates controlled and stable behavior. Watch what you say to them and how you say it. Be careful with your voice tones. Avoid negative comments and sarcasm.

A "*C*" student tends to see a "*D*" teacher as somewhat overbearing, because the "*D*" teacher emphasizes getting the job done, while a "*C*" student emphasizes getting the job done right. The teacher needs to allow these students the time and opportunity for their efforts to be thoroughly thought out. They like to be correct and thorough in their tasks. Be sure to compliment their accomplishments.

The "***D***" Teacher prefers to teach by:

1. Demonstration
2. Visual Aids
3. Experiments
4. Drill
5. Repetition
6. Lecture
7. Competitive Games

Characterizing Traits of "***D***" Teachers:

1. Practical
2. Hard working
3. Structured
4. Well organized
5. To the point, may be too blunt

"***D***" Type Teachers See Education as:

A means to an end. A good education will simply help students to achieve personal success faster and better.

There IS an "*I*" in Team

(AN "***I***" TYPE TEACHER WORKING WITH ***D-I-S-C*** STUDENTS.)

Being a high school physical education teacher and head football coach with an "***I***" type personality style can sometimes be a challenge. I recognize the importance of each athlete's own individual ability. However, I am also well aware of the importance of teamwork. I have learned many valuable lessons over the years about a team, but the biggest one of all came in the form of a play-off game.

Several years ago, our football team made it to the championship game. It was the first time that I had ever coached a team in a championship game, and it was the school's first time to be in the play-offs. Needless to say, we were all excited about the situation. However, the pressure to do our best was hard on me, as well as the team. Things seemed to be very intense for all of us.

In the first half, with the score tied, my team was driving for a go-ahead touchdown. On this specific play, the left guard for our team was supposed to pull to his right to block the opposing team's defensive end. The guard forgot to pull and our quarterback was sacked, but it didn't stop there. Our quarterback fumbled the ball, and their defensive end picked up the ball and returned it for a touchdown!

When halftime rolled around, I knew it was going to be up to me to face our players and to say just the right thing to get them back in the game.

Naturally, I began in my own comfort zone. As an "***I***" type personality, I felt that it was important to tell them not to panic. I let them know that the game would not be determined by only one play, and that we were very much still alive!

Then, I gave the "***D***" players some control. I told them that they needed to be in charge and lead the team down the field.

I reminded the "***I***" type players that this was the game of a lifetime. If we could come from behind and win, we would have the biggest celebration party in the history of our school, and they would all be hometown heroes!

For the "***S***" players, I thanked them for the hard effort they had put forth in the first half. I praised them for specific plays they successfully accomplished and let them know what an excellent job they were doing. I told them how much I appreciated each one of them. (I did not praise them individually.)

For the "**C**" players, I went to the chalkboard and reviewed how our most important plays were supposed to work. I went over, step-by-step, other plays we needed to run in the second half. I reviewed our game plan with them to let them know that we were doing a lot of things right.

When I felt as if I had approached it from every style, we went back onto the field, stronger and more of a team.

We played a beautiful second half. So much, in fact, that we won the game! I must admit that it felt good to be the coach of a championship team, but it felt even better to understand my players, know how to motivate them and get to be the "***I***" in team.

The combination of an "***I***" coach interacting with ***D-I-S-C*** students is illustrated in this story.

The "***I***" coach gave the "***D***" players a sense of control and dominance.

The "***I***" coach displayed optimism and calmness for the "***I***" players to help keep them focused.

The "***I***" coach gave the "***S***" players sincere gratitude and praise.

The "***I***" coach gave the "***C***" players systematic, step-by-step objectives for the second half. He reminded them that the game was not finished.

STRATEGIES AN "*I*" TEACHER SHOULD USE WHEN WORKING WITH ***D-I-S-C*** STUDENTS:

A "***D***" student does not want silliness or informalities from an "***I***" teacher. The teacher should seek to be consistent in his professionalism. Be on guard that the "***D***" student does not take advantage of any inconsistencies or follow-through on your part.

An "***I***" student wants the "***I***" teacher to emphasize the positive. Avoid being critical or negative in approaching the "***I***" student's behavior or efforts. Don't forget to listen to the concerns of the "***I***" students.

An "***S***" student wants an "***I***" teacher to be sincere and appreciative. Publicly acknowledge the achievements and contributions of the "***S***" students as a group. However, do not publicly single out "***S***" students and praise them. Privately compliment them. If possible, add touch, such as a hand on the shoulder to help affirm them. Also, actively seek their help in accomplishing tasks.

A "***C***" student wants an "***I***" teacher to be precise and methodical. When talking to these students, be very specific in your instructions and expectations.

The "*I*" Teacher prefers to teach by:

1. Relating personal experiences (easy to get them off the subject)
2. Collaboration and team teaching
3. Personal discussion (gets everyone involved)
4. Small group tutorials

Characterizing Traits of "*I*" Teachers:

1. Personable
2. Dramatic
3. Energetic
4. Lack of organization in lesson plans
5. Good Natured
6. Outgoing

"*I*" Type teachers See Education as:

An opportunity to learn new things, meet new people and make new friends.

The One That Got Away

(AN "***S***" TYPE TEACHER WORKING WITH ***D-I-S-C*** STUDENTS.)

The longer a teacher stays in education, the more he realizes just how powerful his presence can be in the lives of the students. Teachers have the ability to make or break a child, so to speak. Unfortunately, many times we forget that our ultimate goal is to influence our students not control them. For the most part, that means adjusting our own personalities and expectations. When I think of just how important it is to understand the different personality types, I think of Joseph.

Joseph was a good athlete, and he was definitely an "***I***" type personality. Even with my own easygoing "***S***" type personality, I must admit that Joseph could be a handful at times. I never had any major trouble from Joseph. I believe that it was because I understood him and adjusted my personality to work with his personality. In a couple of other classes, however, Joseph stayed in trouble.

One particular teacher with a "***C***" type personality style had a very difficult time with Joseph. I believe that she felt intimidated by Joseph, and he knew it. I also believe that she was too picky and too structured for Joseph.

Another teacher, a "***D***" type personality, was extremely headstrong. It was either her way or the highway, and Joseph would not budge. These problems eventually led to a special faculty meeting to try to solve this problem.

The principal, also an "***S***" type personality, led the meeting. Joseph, the "***C***" and "***D***" type teachers, and I all attended. The principal and I, with our "***S***" personalities, tried to serve as mediators between Joseph and the two teachers, but the meeting did not go very well. The two teachers were unable to see where or why they needed to make any adjustments. In fact, they accused me of taking Joseph's side over theirs. I wanted to explain to them that there were two sides to everything, and that Joseph had feelings and frustrations, just like they did. However, I saw no sense in adding fuel to the fire.

Two days after the meeting, the "***D***" teacher sent Joseph to the principal's office. Joseph was sent home for the day. The following week, the "***C***" and "***D***" teachers met with Joseph's parents. The end result was not good. Joseph's parents were so upset by the end of the meeting that they immediately pulled Joseph out of school and enrolled him in a private school.

It is sad to think that we lost Joseph. He had many good qualities, as did the "***C***" and "***D***" teachers. It was not an individual failure that led to this sad conclusion but rather a failure of working with one another.

I wish all stories regarding personality types could end successfully. However, that would not be reality or true. In this case, a relatively easy problem to solve turned into a major conflict, simply because it was not handled correctly. Hopefully, reading about this incident will give the reader insight into how to better handle such a situation.

The combination of an "***S***" teacher interacting with ***D-I-S-C*** personalities is illustrated in this story.

The "***S***" teacher was non-confrontational and nice with the "***D***" teacher.

The "***S***" teacher was understanding and empathetic with the "***I***" student.

The "***S***" teacher was loyal and calming with the "***S***" principal.

The "***S***" teacher was withdrawn and intimidated by the "***C***" teacher.

STRATEGIES AN "*S*" TEACHER SHOULD USE WHEN WORKING WITH *D-I-S-C* STUDENTS:

A "*D*" student wants to see confidence and strength in an "*S*" teacher. Be decisive, direct and firm in dealing with "*D*" students.

"*I*" students not only want an "*S*" teacher to listen, but also to share his thoughts and concerns with them. Be honest with your responses to "*I*" students. (However, don't be blinded by their fast-talking charisma that attempts to get you offtrack.)

"*S*" students want an "*S*" teacher to be kind, without overdoing it. Be sincere. If you have negative feelings when dealing with the student, don't ignore these feelings in the hope that the emotions will go away. Deal with the feelings honestly, and encourage the student to do likewise.

"*C*" students want an "*S*" teacher to give concrete answers and assignments. Be systematic and specific about your expectations, including the time frame and desired final results.

The "*S*" Teacher prefers to teach by:

1. Thinking "outside of the box" creatively
2. Role-playing
3. Field trips
4. Creative expression
5. Class consensus
6. "Hands-on" approach
7. Cooperation among students toward the teacher

Characterizing Traits of "*S*" Teachers:

1. Warm
2. Friendly
3. Enthusiastic
4. Innovative
5. Insightful
6. Supportive
7. Sensitive

"*S*" Type Teachers See Education as:

A way to help the world become a nicer place and to help themselves and their students to become better people.

Jurrasic Park?

(A "*C*" TYPE TEACHER WORKING WITH ***D-I-S-C*** STUDENTS.)

Being a "*C*" type teacher of a seventh grade class can be very interesting, to say the least. I tend to analyze and agonize over every decision and every lesson plan. One activity that I put *even* more thought into than usual was the activity that followed our unit on fossils. It was an archeological dig activity.

The dig site would be a pile of Mississippi gravel that had been donated to our school. It was located at the far back corner of the building. The students would dig for two days and keep notes. Then, we would construct a classroom museum in which to display our fossils. I knew that this was going to be the best project of the year.

I began to give exact and thorough instructions as to the specific, proper procedures to use and the type of fossils that we were seeking. During my instructions, David, a "***D***" type personality, said, "Can't we just go? We all know what to do." It was difficult for me not to get defensive.

I turned my attention to Carla, an "***I***" type personality. She was talking a mile a minute, telling anyone who would listen about a movie she saw in which two teens were digging for fossils and uncovered a mummy. She, then, began walking like a mummy and chasing Cody, a "***C***" type personality. My patience was short with Carla. I did not feel like dealing with her antics. I had to remind myself to be patient with Carla and to overlook her immaturity. It seemed like she needed my constant attention to stay on track.

Once the students began digging and unearthing their fossils, I noticed Tim, an "***S***" type personality, walking around with a large plastic bag. He had taken it upon himself to hold the bag while others put their fossils into it. Even though I knew the fossils were going to get mixed up in that one bag, I thanked Tim for his help, rather than pointing out the inevitable confusion that would soon follow.

As the students continued digging, I heard Cody briefing everyone on the proper techniques to use for excavating archeological digs. He was precise and accurate, and he actually did a much better job of explaining all the details to the other students than I ever could do.

As our dig came to an end and we headed back to class, I stood away from the group and took inventory. David was leading the group back to the room quickly and efficiently. Cody was walking and reading the notes he had taken on all of the different fossils that he had uncovered. Carla had placed one of the bones she dug up in her hair and was doing a wonderful impression of Pebbles from "The Flintstones." Tim was his calm, helpful self. I was just thankful that the day was almost finished, and I wondered how I was ever going to get that bone out of Carla's hair.

The combination of a "**C**" teacher interacting with ***D-I-S-C*** students is illustrated in this story.

The "**C**" teacher and the "***D***" student tend to clash over doing tasks. The "***D***" student wants to jump right in, whereas the "**C**" teacher wants to think things through and move ahead a little slower.

The "**C**" teacher has a difficult time understanding the "***I***" student's constant need for fun and socialization.

The "**C**" teacher is frequently too critical of the "***S***" student's lack of attention to detail or level of achievement.

The "**C**" teacher and the "**C**" student can be a natural combination, until they disagree on something. Then, both believe they are right, and this can result in them avoiding each other.

STRATEGIES A "*C*" TEACHER SHOULD USE WHEN WORKING WITH *D-I-S-C* STUDENTS:

"***D***" students have a naturally fast pace, but they rarely think things through. Help them to pay closer attention to the details and to be more careful and conscientious in their work habits.

"***I***" students have social recognition and approval as their greatest motivations. Publicly praise and acknowledge their achievements and contributions often.

"***S***" students are sensitive and will not thrive under harsh or consistent criticism. This will "shut them down" and make them feel insecure. They will then become unproductive. Be gentle and sensitive when dealing with them.

"***C***" students will wage a war of indirect, quiet communication when upset. They are very controlling of the external expression of their emotions. They dislike direct confrontation and conflict. However, they will communicate their displeasure with you in a subtle manner.

The "**C**" Teacher prefers to teach by:

1. Lecture
2. Focused discussion
3. Debate
4. Examination
5. Inquiry
6. Inspection
7. Scientific Experimentation

Characterizing Traits of "**C**" Teachers:

1. Logical
2. Persistent
3. Ingenious
4. Systematic
5. Thorough
6. Serious-minded

"**C**" Type Teachers See Education as:

A serious matter. To them, the future and betterment of mankind depends upon useful knowledge and information.

ADDITIONAL INSIGHTS FOR UNDERSTANDING ***DISC*** STUDENTS

Classroom Climate

Every teacher creates a climate in the classroom. One teacher may be a strong disciplinarian with a *military base* classroom, while the teacher next door is a sensitive nurse with a *hospital* classroom. The teacher on the other side of the hall is a clown with a classroom that is similar to a *playground*.

The question is not which climate is best. Most educators can defend their environment preferences. The solution is in creating a climate or engineering several environments that encourage every student to learn at his best.

One student needs a dictatorial General Patton teacher, while another student needs a merciful Nurse Nightingale. Every child has a unique personality that affects his results.

The most effective educator knows how to motivate each student according to the student's personality. The biggest mistake some teachers make is trying to lead every student according to the teacher's personality.

Most teachers know that every student is different, but under pressure, many teachers forget. The result is that each of those teachers motivate the whole class according to the teacher's temperament.

The following pages have simple descriptions of specific personality types. Study each type and develop strategies to improve your effectiveness. Think of specific times when you might have responded better. Develop strategies to work with specific students.

"*D*" TYPE TEACHERS:

Under Pressure They:

Become determined, decisive, driving, serious, challenging and a disciplinarian

Sources of Irritation:

1. Silliness and insecurity
2. Overly cautiousness people
3. Lack of: initiative, competitiveness, aggressiveness, assertiveness and confidence

They Need To:

1. Think before acting
2. Meet demands with clear answers
3. Be loyal
4. Pay attention to details
5. Inspire others through charm and friendliness

"*I*" TYPE TEACHERS:

Under Pressure They:

Become silly, manipulative, restless, wordy (they talk too much) and they seek attention

Sources of Irritation:

1. Dullness and deadness
2. Status quo and predictability
3. Restrictive communication and quietness
4. Lack of encouragement
5. Pessimism and negativism

They Need To:

1. Use silence to express displeasure
2. Appreciate the team effort
3. Take complaints seriously
4. Focus on details
5. Use hard facts to prove points

"*S*" TYPE TEACHERS:

Under Pressure They:

Become silent, nervous, shy and they take blame that they are not responsible for and do whatever is necessary to please others

Sources of Irritation:

1. Aggression and competition
2. Undependable people
3. Impatience and insincerity
4. Inconsistency
5. Having to look good
6. Pressure to speak out

They Need To:

1. Be more spontaneous, active and mobile
2. Be inspiring
3. Be more demanding, determined and confrontational
4. Verbalize feelings
5. Take risks

"*C*" TYPE TEACHERS:

Under Pressure They:

Become picky, critical, unsociable, worrisome, questioning and they dig deeper into things

Sources of Irritation:

1. Incomplete reports and careless mistakes
2. Thoughtless work and illogical responses
3. Inaccurate facts and unclear answers
4. Foolishness

They Need To:

1. Improve people skills
2. Be enthusiastic, positive and caring
3. Be sensitive and decisive
4. Allow others to learn by their mistakes

Encourage Others

Strengths

Fortunately, each personality type possesses special abilities:

"***D***s": Confidence, Ability to take charge

"***I***s": Impressive, Influencing

"***S***s": Serving, Sharing, Obedience

"***C***s": Analysis, Correction

Weaknesses/"Uniquenesses"

Unfortunately, each personality type possesses special disabilities:

"***D***s": Impatience, Insensitivity

"***I***s": Pride, Talks too much

"***S***s": Gives in, Too nice

"***C***s": Critical, Worrisome, Excessive questioning

Motivating Students

Most children need discipline. Dealing with disobedient and disruptive students can be challenging. Public correction can either help or hurt students. Knowing what works best often depends on knowing each student's personality type.

Discipline must be motivating. All children have "hot buttons" that ignite them. Students also have "cold buttons" that turn them off. A teacher's personal "hot button" can be a certain student's "cold button." In other words, things that motivate the teacher may, in fact, do just the opposite for a student.

WE CANNOT MOTIVATE OTHERS

There is a misconception about motivation - that we can motivate others. The truth is that people are already motivated... to do exactly what they want to do!

Everyone is motivated. Some students are motivated to do one thing, while others are motivated to do the exact opposite, but everyone is motivated.

"Motivation" is actually creating the climate and environment that makes students decide for themselves to do what is right. Unfortunately, many teachers discipline and motivate through intimidation and manipulation.

Effective teaching involves wise discipline that creates the climate to motivate each child individually. The following are suggestions on how to motivate/discipline students according to their personalities.

Remember, what motivates you may not motivate a student. Think of certain students who may respond better by your using different approaches.

"*D*" TYPE STUDENTS:

Under Pressure They:

Become resistant, rebellious, strong-willed, angry, stubborn, demanding and controlling

Sources of Irritation:

1. Weakness and losing
2. Indecisiveness and laziness
3. Lack of: leadership, discipline and challenges

To Motivate/Discipline:

1. Establish and remind – "I'm the boss!"
2. Give opportunity to lead the class to the cafeteria or with a special project or be a captain of a team
3. Give one warning, then follow through with discipline
4. When disobedient, put them last in line
5. Sit out during a challenging game

"*I*" TYPE STUDENTS:

Under Pressure They:

Become active, impatient and loud; they seek attention, excitement and to please the crowd

Sources of Irritation:

1. Boredom and routine
2. Being overlooked
3. Criticism and time constraints
4. Organizational demands

To Motivate/Discipline:

1. Recognize (videotape) good behavior
2. Give opportunity to express their thoughts
3. Show your grave displeasure with their poor behavior
4. When disobedient, exclude from activities
5. Explain how poor behavior makes them look bad
   Relate popularity to responsibility

"*S*" TYPE STUDENTS:

Under Pressure They:

Become submissive or stubborn - depending on the threat to security; they seek stability, friendships, status quo and peace

Sources of Irritation:

1. Intimidation and inflexibility
2. Turmoil and disloyalty
3. Insincerity and pride
4. Discrimination and unfairness

To Motivate/Discipline:

1. Establish close relationship – Be friends
2. Emphasize need for help
3. Appreciate loyalty
4. Give time to prepare and adjust
5. When disobedient, show heartfelt hurt
6. Don't "rub-in" wrong actions. Show silent disapproval

"*C*" TYPE STUDENTS:

Under Pressure They:

Become uptight, faultfinding, pessimistic, critical, worrisome, overly cautious, technical, picky and they will go by the book

Sources of Irritation:

1. Uncertainty and incompetence
2. Disorganization and simplicity
3. Dishonesty and inaccuracy

To Motivate/Discipline:

1. Explain reasons for desired action
2. Allow questions and suggestions to improve
3. Give opportunity to research and evaluate
4. When disobedient, prohibit opportunity to analyze and/or correct serious problems
5. Write reasons why obedience is important

TEACHER/STUDENT CONFLICTS

Conflicts between students and teachers are inevitable. It's often the same students that constantly conflict with teachers. It's also the same teachers that don't seem to handle conflicts well.

Understanding students' personalities will help you to deal with the differences. Learn to identify students' motivations – why they think, feel and act the way they do.

Students sometimes have totally different personalities from their parents. An aggressive parent may have a passive child. Don't think that the parent will be just like the student. Learn to deal with students according to their specific personalities.

As a professional, it's your responsibility to adapt and control the conflict. Don't expect the parent to do so.

The following are the basic motivations of students:

"*D*" Type students:

D

1. They want to control.
2. They want to win.
3. They want to be challenged.
4. They want to rise above the crowd.
5. They want to be leaders, tough and confident.
6. They do not want to be taken advantage of or feel weak.

"*I*" Type students:

1. They want to look good.
2. They want to receive recognition and positive strokes.
3. They want to stand out.
4. They want to reach their potential and develop their talents.

"*S*" Type students:

1. They want secure classroom environments.
2. They want to be taught with sensitivity and steadiness.
3. They want to be safe.
4. They don't like turmoil and change.

"*C*" Type students:

1. They want competent teachers.
2. They want to receive answers to all their questions.
3. They want to stretch their intellect.
4. They want to calculate, contemplate and be cautious.

 Type Teacher Having Conflict With

"***D***" Student (*the teacher should know*):

1. Be strong but willing to bend.
2. Get to the point.
3. Show your goal and plan to help the student.
4. The student may challenge and intimidate.

"***I***" Student (*the teacher should know*):

1. Be enthusiastic and complimentary.
2. Control the conversation, but allow him to express himself.
3. The student will talk and exaggerate a lot.

"***S***" Student (*the teacher should know*):

1. Be sweet.
2. Don't be forceful or speak down.
3. Be sensitive and kind.
4. Appreciate the student's concerns.
5. The student will judge how your respond.

"***C***" Student (*the teacher should know*):

1. Be prepared.
2. Don't use generalities.
3. Be specific.
4. Give explanations not hype.
5. The student can be stubborn, if he senses you are incompetent.

 Type Teacher Having Conflict With

"***D***" **Student (*the teacher should know*):**

1. Be serious.
2. Don't be silly or informal.
3. Don't waste time.
4. Demonstrate your plan of action.
5. The student is interested in action; the student. is not interested in funny stories.

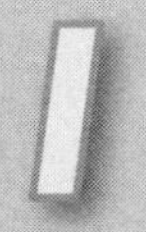

"***I***" **Student (*the teacher should know*):**

1. Be a good listener.
2. Don't talk much.
3. Compliment the student.
4. Emphasize the good and positive.
5. Smile and be enthusiastic.

"***S***" **Student (*the teacher should know*):**

1. Be sensitive.
2. Stay calm and reinforce your sensitivity.
3. Let the student share his concern.
4. Let the student finish completely.
5. Don't interrupt.

"***C***" **Student (*the teacher should know*):**

1. Be factual.
2. Don't try to "snow" the student.
3. Ask for suggestions.
4. Be open and respectful.
5. Give details concerning the problem.
6. Be precise and methodical.

 Type Teacher Having Conflict With

"**D**" Student (*the teacher should know*):

1. Be confident and sure of yourself.
2. Show strength.
3. Challenge the student.
4. Don't give in if you know you're right.
5. The student may be forceful.

"***I***" Student (*the teacher should know*):

1. Be interested in what the student says.
2. Don't just listen. Share your thoughts and concerns.
3. Ask the student to review what he hears.

"***S***" Student (*the teacher should know*):

1. Be kind, but don't overdo it.
2. Be strong, if necessary.
3. Don't hold back, but be sensitive.
4. Encourage the student to be stronger concerning his problems.

"**C**" Student (*the teacher should know*):

1. Be ready for stress.
2. Give concrete answers.
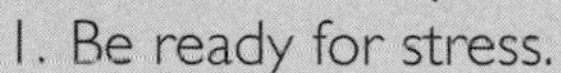
3. Be open to what is said.
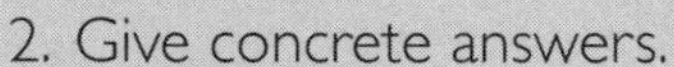
4. Be cautiously optimistic.
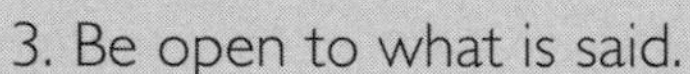
5. The student will pressure you with logic or reasons.

Type Teacher Having Conflict With

"***D***" Student (*the teacher should know*):

1. Be relaxed.
2. Don't be defensive.
3. Get to the "bottom line."
4. Don't bore the student with a lot of facts.
5. Design a solution based on both perspectives.
6. Be positive.

"***I***" Student (*the teacher should know*):

1. Be patient.
2. Let the student talk.
3. Ask pointed questions that make the student think.
4. Get the student to talk through the solution.
5. Stay on track.

S

"***S***" Student (*the teacher should know*):

1. Be loving.
2. Show sincere care for the student.
3. Make the student feel that you really enjoy what you do.
4. Don't complain.
5. Be optimistic and sure of your plan.

"***C***" Student (*the teacher should know*):

1. Be precise and accurate.
2. Meet forceful demands with clear answers.
3. Be sure of your facts. Be open to suggestions.
4. The student may be right.

INSIGHTS ON DISCIPLINE FOR TEACHERS

The most effective disciplining is accomplished when teachers adapt their personalities to that of the students. Being able to identify a student's predictable patterns of behavior will improve results.

Knowing how to uniquely respond to the different students styles is so valuable. Every personality type obviously responds according to his feelings, thoughts and motivations.

Disciplining friends can also become difficult. Familiarity often breeds contempt. In other words, the closer you get, the easier it is to conflict. The things we love about someone, we can begin to despise.

Understanding Human Behavior Science will help you deal with the differences between you and others in discipline situations.

An aggressive discipliner can overwhelm a passive student. Don't think the student will respond just like you do. Learn to deal with students according to their specific personalities.

The following are proven and practical ways to deal with different types of disciplees' personalities. Focus on **your** "***D***", "***I***", "***S***" or "***C***" type, along with that personality style of the student you need to correct. In addition, be sure to consider the qualities you possess from your personality blend.

"*Ds*" ***DISC***iplining

"**D**s":

1. Get to the point
2. Challenge
3. Give choices
4. Clarify chain of command
5. Don't give ultimatums
6. Don't force issues
7. Show meekness – power under control

"***I***s":

1. Relax
2. Have more fun
3. Be enthusiastic and complimentary
4. Listen more
5. Don't be controlling
6. Praise
7. Encourage results

"***S***s":

1. Be kind and sensitive
2. Build confidence
3. Teach boldness and assertiveness
4. Be patient, but persistent
5. Don't belittle
6. Constantly reaffirm

"**C**s":

1. Answer questions
2. Give homework
3. Avoid being negative
4. Give opportunities to evaluate
5. Expect objections
6. Give practical steps of action

"*I*s" ***DISC***iplining

"***D***s":

1. Build respect
2. Be strong
3. Don't waste time
4. Don't talk too much
5. Give clear direction
6. Challenge
7. Model spiritual discipline

"***I***s":

1. Take turns talking
2. Praise more than seeking to be praised
3. Be careful what you promise
4. Listen well
5. Be punctual and conscientious

"***S***s":

1. Don't control conversations
2. Give opportunity to express self
3. Give times to adjust
4. Take small steps of action
5. Encourage boldness

"***C***s":

1. Be prepared
2. Don't expect instant positive responses
3. Give time to evaluate
4. Don't exaggerate
5. Be accurate and systematic

"*Ss*" *DISC*iplining

"*D*s":
1. Demand respect and establish authority
2. Be strong enough to confront and correct
3. Be assertive and aggressive
4. Don't be too nice or weak-willed

"*I*s":
1. Demand respect and establish authority
2. Be strong enough to confront and correct
3. Be assertive and aggressive
4. Don't be too nice or weak-willed

"*S*s":
1. Appeal to logic
2. Be positive and reassuring
3. Don't be intimidated
4. Give practical reasons for action
5. Initiate response
6. Don't withdraw
7. Be more demanding

"*C*s":
1. Appeal to logic
2. Encourage risk-taking
3. Model assertiveness and boldness
4. Communicate optimism
5. Demonstrate strength
6. Be decisive, yet patient

"*Cs*" *DISC*iplining

"*D*s":

1. Be positive and optimistic
2. Don't overdo teaching and explanations
3. Allow opportunities to be on their own
4. Don't try to control
5. Don't criticize
6. Create dreams

"*I*s":

1. Be expressive
2. Don't be picky
3. Let them talk, but you should control conversations
4. Don't give too many study assignments
5. Be upbeat and happy

"*S*s":

1. Be sweet and sensitive
2. Don't be faultfinding
3. Don't be too hard on them
4. Recognize the little things they do well
5. Give lots of praise
6. Reassure, but stretch

"*C*s":

1. Be methodical, but don't get bogged down in the details
2. Set optimistic goals
3. Encourage risk-taking
4. Teach the big picture
5. Be more results-oriented

PERSONALITY COMBINATION GRAPHS

(Two personality styles working together)

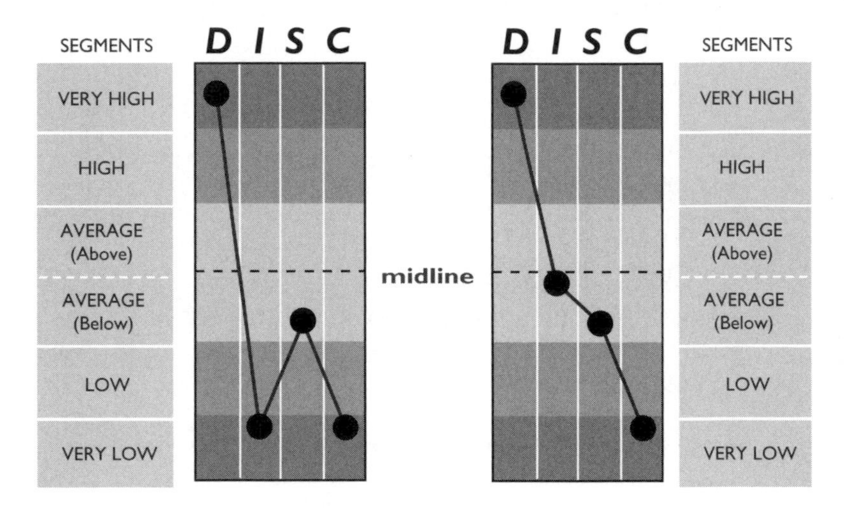

Classroom Index: Two "***D***s" can teach and learn well together as long as the "***D***" student recognizes the "***D***" teacher is the "boss." "***D***" students must respect and trust their "***D***" teacher or there will be conflicts. Two "***D***s" will struggle over control and authority. They must learn to give-and-take. "***D***" teachers must learn when and how to give "***D***" students liberty to decide for themselves.

Practical Application:

1. Establish your authority early.
2. Allow students to become leaders.
3. Give choices, not ultimatums.
4. Clearly define limits.
5. Slow down in making decisions.
6. Learn to control yourself first.
7. Learn to relax and control stress levels.

"**D**"/"**I**" or "**I**"/"**D**"

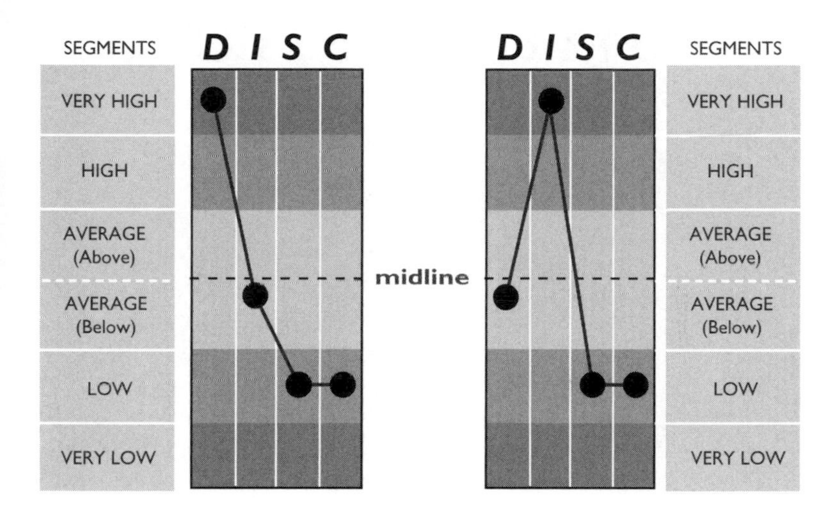

Classroom Index: "**D**s" and "**I**s" teaching and learning together result in a lot of activity. The "**D**" wants to control, while the "**I**" wants to impress. The "**I**" wants to talk, while the "**D**" works. The "**D**" tends to dominate, while the "**I**" desires to communicate. The "**I**" feels the "**D**" doesn't care, while the "**D**" thinks the "**I**" is too sensitive. "**D**s" are too serious, while "**I**s" are too impulsive.

Practical Application:

1. Determine to communicate on the basis of the other person's needs.
2. Don't intimidate or manipulate.
3. "**D**s" need to show that they really care.
4. "**I**s" need to give "**D**s" a chance to talk.
5. "**D**s" should praise "**I**s" more.
6. "**I**s" should be more industrious.

"***D***"/"***S***" or "***S***"/"***D***"

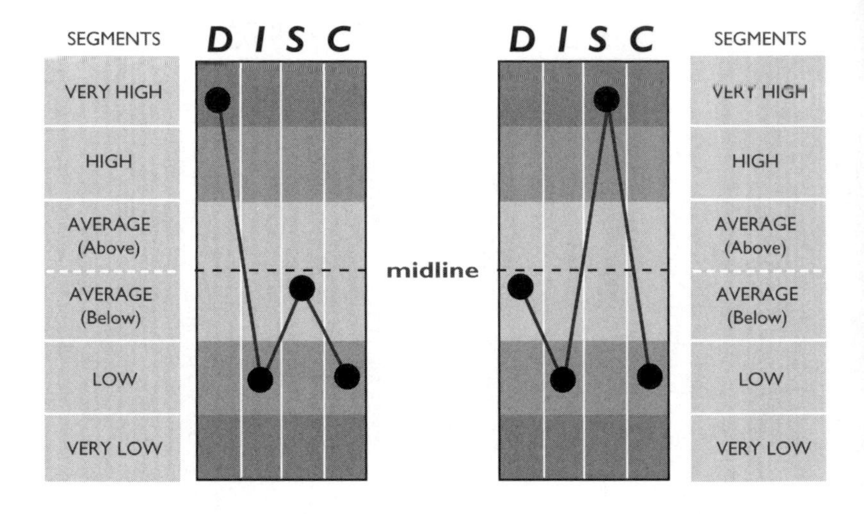

Classroom Index: "***D***s" and "***S***s" teaching and learning together can be like masters and slaves. "***D***s" try to tell "***S***s" what to do. "***D***s" need to appreciate "***S***s" for their hard work. "***D***s" try to dominate "***S***s" but should never take them for granted. "***S***s" feel secure with "***D***s" as long as "***D***s" show controlled and stable behavior. "***S***s" should be more assertive; "***D***s" should be more compromising.

Practical Application:

1. "***D***s" should not try to dominate "***S***s".
2. When the "***D***" is out of control, the "***S***" should be careful.
3. "***S***s" need to strongly appeal to "***D***s" when their behavior is unacceptable.
4. "***S***s" should show more determination.
5. "***S***" teachers must take charge.

"**D**"/"**C**" or "**C**"/"**D**"

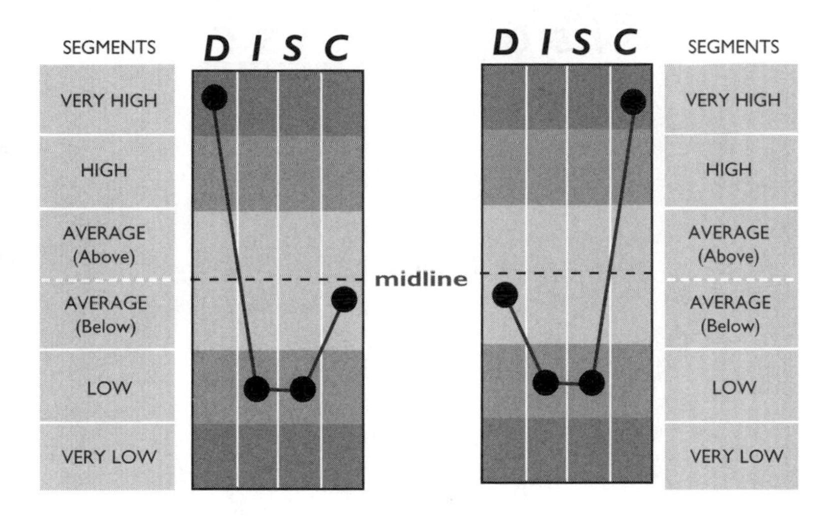

Classroom Index: A "**D**" and "**C**" teaching and learning together may conflict over dreams and details. The "**D**" wants to get the job done, while the "**C**" wants to get it done right. "**D**s" and "**C**s" are both task-oriented. "**D**s" are optimistic, while "**C**s" are more pessimistic (realistic). "**D**s" need to be more careful, while "**C**s" need to be more positive.

Practical Application:

1. Be more understanding of the other's perspective.
2. Allow others to feel the way they feel.
3. "**D**s" ought to listen more to "**C**s".
4. "**C**s" should avoid always being negative.
5. Give "**C**s" chances to think about decisions.
6. "**C**s" need to take more risks; "**D**s" need to be more careful.

"*I*" / "*I*"

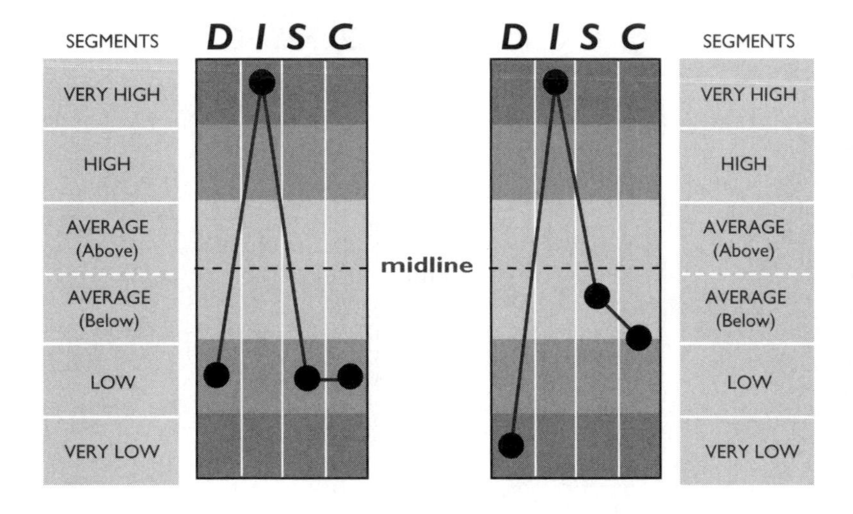

Classroom Index: Two high "*I*s" teaching and learning together will talk more than work. They compete for praise and approval. They tend to be overly optimistic and enthusiastic. Two "*I*s" communicate well, if one doesn't out-talk the other. "*I*s" need to remember that communication goes two ways – talking and listening. Each wants attention. Both tend to be emotional.

Practical Application:

1. Take turns talking.
2. "*I*s" don't listen well; ask the other to repeat back what he heard.
3. Write down what you agreed upon, so there will be no misunderstandings.
4. Praise each other more than seeking to be praised.

"*I*"/"*D*" is on page 155.

"*I*"/"*S*" or "*S*"/"*I*"

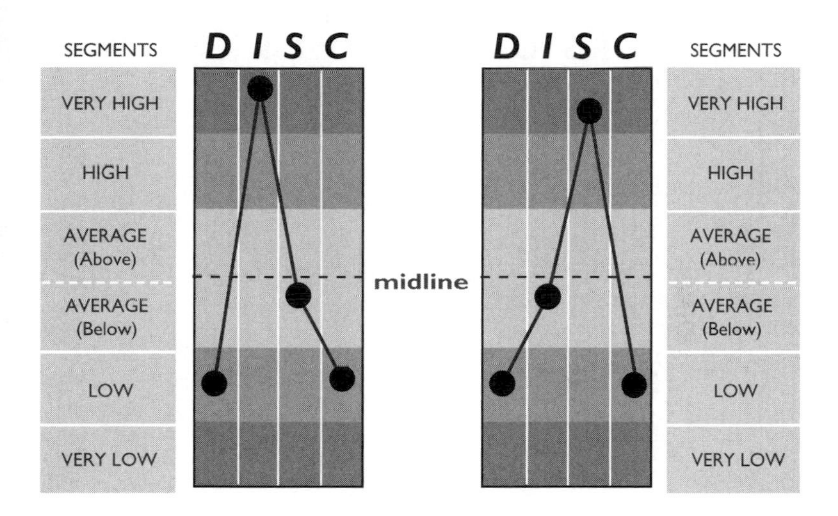

Classroom Index: "***I***s" and "***S***s" don't tend to be task-oriented. They would rather "relate" with others. "***I***s" are great talkers, while "***S***s" listen well. "***I***s" and "***S***s" are both people-oriented. "***I***s" love excitement, while "***S***s" are more shy. "***I***s" want "***S***s" to be more enthusiastic, but "***S***s" don't like a lot of attention. "***I***s" love crowds; "***S***s" prefer small groups.

Practical Application:

1. When an "***I***" asks an "***S***" a question, the "***I***" should wait for the "***S***" to answer.
2. "***S***s" shouldn't let "***I***s" always interrupt and control every conversation.
3. "***S***s" should ask "***I***s" to repeat what "***S***s" have said.
4. "***I***s" tend to think of what they want to say next rather than listening closely.

"*I*"/"*C*" or "*C*"/"*I*"

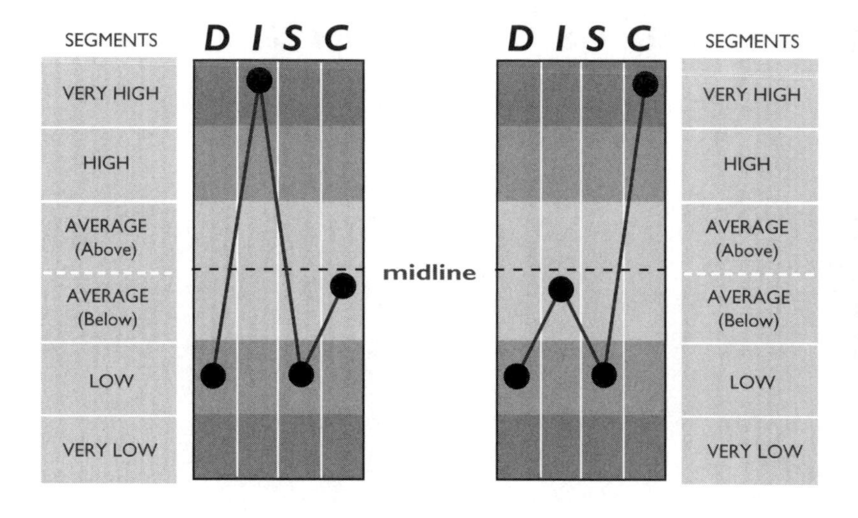

Classroom Index: "*I*s" and "**C**s" make good teachers and learners, when "*I*s" explain and "**C**s" become more optimistic. "*I*s" dislike the "**C**s" pessimism, while "**C**s" distrust the "*I*s" facts. "*I*s" and "**C**s" often don't understand each other. "*I*s" are more active, while "**C**s" are more passive. "*I*s" are feeling-oriented, while "**C**s" are task-oriented. They are definitely opposite but can complement each other.

Practical Application:

1. "*I*s" need to trust "**C**s" concerns.
2. "**C**s" ought to be more optimistic about "*I*s" interests.
3. "*I*s" should be thoroughly prepared before trying to convince "**C**s" about a fact.
4. "**C**s" need to express themselves instead of internally criticizing "*I*s".

"**S**" / "**S**"

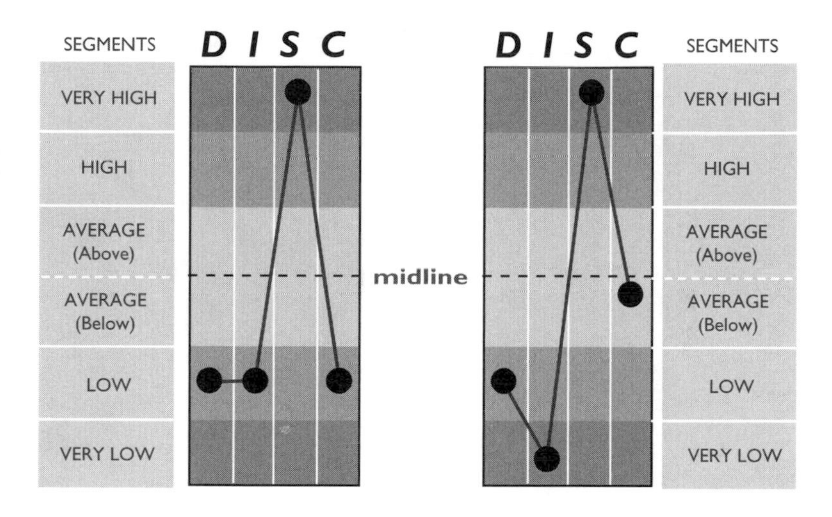

Classroom Index: Two high "**S**s" relate well. They don't compete or criticize each other. They are loyal and sensitive. They make great teachers and learners. "**S**s" are the most tolerant and forgiving types. They are not assertive, and they struggle with making decisions. If they are not careful, others will take advantage of them. They need to be more bold, exciting and competent.

Practical Application:

1. Try not to depend on the other for major decisions.
2. Be more enthusiastic and outgoing.
3. Don't miss great opportunities, because you don't want to take risks.
4. Force yourself to express your feelings.

"***S***"/"***D***" is on page 156.
"***S***"/"***I***" is on page 159.

"S"/"C" or "C"/"S"

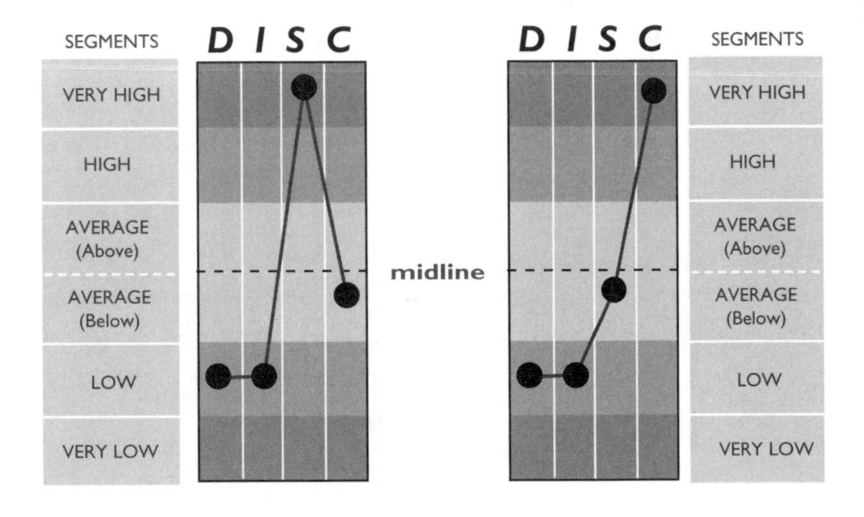

Classroom Index: "**S**s" and "**C**s" teaching and learning together will result in a passive and methodical environment. Precision and propriety come before performance. "**S**s" want "**C**s" to be more friendly. "**S**s" want "**C**s" to be less picky. "**S**s" are generally more forgiving than"**C**s". "**S**s" desire more intimacy, while "**C**s" prefer their projects. They are both quiet and private. They can coexist with little conversation.

Practical Application:

1. "**S**s" need to be more precise with "**C**s".
2. "**C**s" must be more friendly with "**S**s".
3. "**S**s" should appeal to "**C**s" logic.
4. Be more caring and aggressive.
5. Be more optimistic and positive.
6. Don't wait on others to express themselves.

"C" / "C"

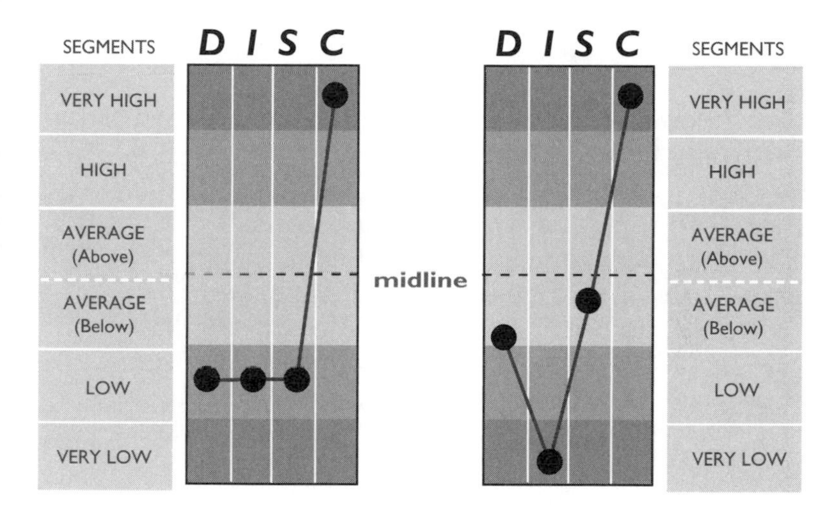

Classroom Index: Two high "**C**s" teaching and learning together can be challenging. Both have high standards for how to do things. "**C**s" tend to think that their way is best. Two "**C**s" will conflict over "right and wrong." They can also be cold and pessimistic. "**C**s" tend to be picky perfectionists and insightful critics. They can be more effective when they are enthusiastic, decisive and kind.

Practical Application:

1. Be more complimentary of each other.
2. Be more expressive and positive.
3. Be more outgoing and people-oriented.
4. Before you speak, think twice about how you want to express what you think.
5. Compromise your way of doing things.
6. Don't criticize each other.
7. Don't keep your feelings inside you.

"***C***"/"***D***" is on page 157.
"***C***"/"***I***" is on page 160.
"***C***"/"***S***" is on page 162.

The following section (pages165-213) was developed and written by Pete Hinojosa.

Pete Hinojosa is a Human Behavior Consultant through Personality Insights, Inc. He has been educating youth since 1992. Pete was recognized three times as an *Outstanding Secondary Educator in the Nation* as well as five times for *Who's Who in American High School Teachers.* He is currently working as the Community Coordinator for Spring Branch Independent School District in Houston, Texas, where he speaks to students and families in fourteen schools. He is a gifted teacher and seminar speaker.

How to Teach to the Four Personalities

Introduction

As I was presenting a high school biology class lecture, I pulled down the overhead screen. To my surprise, there was an unfamiliar sound, and I could not get the screen to stay down. I tried more than once to get the screen to work. In fact, I tried about ten times, using every teacher trick in the book. I pulled out a little at a time - no good. I pulled it out all the way and jiggled it - still no good. I finally gave in and stated the obvious, "I think the screen is broken."

This is when I could see clearly, through the responses of four of my students, the different personalities operating in my classroom. The first response was from my very determined "***D***"student. He said, "You're not doing it right. Let me do it." He grabbed the screen. He pulled it up and down; he jiggled it. He tried everything and then turned to look back at me and mumbled, "Uh, Mr. Hinojosa, I think the screen is broken."

I thought to myself, "No kidding."

The second response was from my energetic, outgoing "***I***" student. He yelled, "FREE DAY!" I began to feel sweat on my shirt and brow. I knew I had to do something and do it fast.

The third response came from my very concerned, task-oriented and reserved "**C**" student. She commented, "Why don't you just write it on the board, because I don't want to get behind the other classes."

The final response came after class ended. My very sweet, reserved but people-oriented student, put her hand on my shoulder as she left the classroom and said, "It's okay.

We all have bad days. I think you recovered great. See you tomorrow."

You are probably well aware, perhaps painfully so, that there are different personalities in your classroom. What you may not know is how to build on that awareness. Although I knew about various personality styles when I began teaching, it was not until I met Dr. Robert Rohm, a gifted communicator, that I began to relate that information to my students. I began to read and study more about personalities and put what I learned into action in my classroom. It made an immediate difference. I developed, over time, a new approach to helping my students succeed.

A New Approach to Student Success –

Step One

Make it different. Don't do what they expect!

The first day of class in my classroom is always different from other classes my students are in. I have them form a single line - in alphabetical order. The students want normal class seating arrangements, but I want their experience in my classroom to be different from the start.

As the students line up, they must introduce themselves to everyone in the class. Then, I have them take a lap around my room to keep them off balance. They cannot be sure what is coming next, but it begins to make sense as they come back around the room. All of the papers are placed on a lab table. As they come around, they can, one at a time, pick up the papers they need for the first week of school. Remember that they are in alphabetical order. So as they take their seats, they, without a seating chart, sit in order. Things begin to make more sense to the students as they are seated.

This is, of course, my way of making the classroom experience different for students. Use your imagination and creativity to come up with something that suits your subject and personality.

Step Two

Get to know your students.

The second aspect of my plan is to spend the next ten minutes learning each student's name. This is a crucial step in building relationships with students. I practice remembering names, so that I can learn the first names of each student in the class in the first ten minutes.

Three tips for remembering student names:

1. After each student tells you his name, repeat the name. Then ask each of them a question.

For example:

"Hi! What's your name?"

"Cynthia Smith."

"Cynthia Smith. Hi, Cynthia. What school did you go to last year, Cynthia?"

"Riverwood"

"Really? That's great! What is your favorite subject, Cynthia?"

2. Learn first names first - Do not try to learn their first and last names on the first day!

3. Be actively interested in learning your students' names. Have you ever noticed how quickly you learn the names of students who cause trouble? Why? Because you want the students to understand that you know who they are if they cause trouble again. Why not turn that attitude around and get to know all of your students by name? It makes a tremendous difference. This seems like a simple and obvious step, but you would not believe how many teachers, even after a full semester, do not know all of their students by name.

Step Three

Introduce your students to the four personalities of ***D I S*** and ***C*** .

The stage is set, after steps one and two, to introduce the third and most important part of my plan. When I am doing a ***DISC*** presentation, I begin with introducing the personalities by giving a brief introduction of the "***D***", "***I***", "***S***" and "***C***" types. At some point during my presentation, someone always stops me and asks what the Japanese symbols on my whiteboard represent. The symbols on my board (purposely put there) are there for two reasons. First, the symbols are an introduction to the scientific method (Observation and State the Problem). Second, the symbols have a specific meaning - they are a Japanese proverb which translated says, "To ask is but a moment's shame, but not to ask and remain ignorant is a lifelong shame."

I want my students to realize that the primary reason that they are in school is to learn. Above all, I want them to feel confident, safe and secure for at least the one hour a day that they are in my classroom. They can feel this confidence by asking questions without feeling stupid or scared. They can feel safe and secure because they can act and feel like themselves without worrying about what others think of them - especially other students. Each of my students is unique and talented. If I can help them better understand their own value in the process of learning science, I feel successful as a teacher.

What does all of this mean to you? As a teacher, you bring your background, viewpoint, emotions, expectations, habits, culture, age-related preferences and personality type into your classroom. You bring your own style. Your students also bring their own styles. Your style greatly influences how you relate to your students, and your students' styles greatly influence how they relate to you.

If you feel like some of your students are just "out to get you," you are not alone. It can feel that way. However, in most instances, those students are simply operating out of their own styles, without a thought about how those styles may conflict with your style.

Ask yourself how well your teaching style fits with each one of your students. Is there a difference in fit with one child compared to another? In other words, does your personality fit with some students and not with others? It is natural for a teacher to communicate and get along with students who are like them. Take a close look at each of your students. Each one is unique - different from all the rest.

Do you really expect everyone in your classroom to think and behave like you? As a teacher, you would never assume that all of your students are exactly the same - with the same needs, desires, strengths and weaknesses. So why would you treat every student the same?

As a teacher, it is important to learn to accept your students' differences instead of criticizing them. No matter how different, or how difficult your students seem to be, you must be the one willing to make the adjustments. In most instances, your students cannot make, or do not know how to make, adjustments themselves. As you discern what it takes to help your students, you will be able to guide them to make adjustments in their own lives. Studying this manual will help you learn to compliment and enjoy your students for who they are.

In his book, *What Do You Really Want for Your Children,* Dr. Wayne W. Dyers says it succinctly:

"People, including your spouse, your children, your parents or anyone else - will never be the way you want them to be. When you find yourself upset with someone else, you are really saying to yourself. 'If only you were thinking the way I am thinking right now, then I wouldn't have to be so upset.' Or 'Why can't you do things the way I want them to be done?'"

The truth of the matter is this:

> You cannot control anyone other than yourself. If you can accomplish this feat, you are doing well! If you can do that, you will have the greatest opportunity to have a good influence in the lives of your students.

As a teacher you well know that knowledge is power. The area of personality styles is no different. The more you learn about dealing with various personalities, the better you will be able to handle your students and the better teacher you will become.

For a classroom to experience harmony and unity, you as a teacher must be willing to make some important adjustments in your natural teaching style and begin to cater to each student as an individual. It is important to note that adjusting your teaching style does not mean becoming a different person. It does, however, mean that you voluntarily and temporarily adjust your behavior in order to meet your students' needs. This requires that you, as a teacher, understand both your own and your students' behavior styles, and that you make adjustments to them as you see the need.

Most problems in the classroom occur from differences in

perception. So you need to be able to recognize how your personal perceptions confuse, color or cloud critical people issues. Your needs, values, self-concept, past experiences, prejudices, likes and dislikes will all influence your perceptions about your students. And yes, your personality style will also influence your perceptions.

Your perceptions can PREVENT you from working effectively with your students.
Your perceptions can PREVENT you from seeing obvious differences in your students.
Your perceptions can INFLUENCE how you view each of your students.

You may perceive differences in students as weaknesses, but you can learn to view your students in terms of their strengths rather than their limitations. The natural tendency for most teachers is just the opposite - to view students in terms of their limitations. And, when a student's perceptions and behavior are not like theirs, teachers naturally think the student is wrong.

Example:

A high "***D***" teacher may wonder why his high "***S***" students are so timid and shy.

A high "***I***" teacher may think his high "***C***" students spend too much time asking questions.

A high "***S***" teacher may want to know why his high "***D***" students aren't already on ritalin.

A high "***C***" teacher, who likes to keep his classroom in perfect order, may be totally exasperated with high "***I***" students who don't seem to care about order "like they should."

These teachers may find themselves constantly frustrated

with the same students, especially those students who have opposite personality styles from their own.

As you learn more about your students, you will be able to adjust your approach and relate to your students according to their needs, not yours. As you learn what encourages your students, what motivates them and how to communicate with them, you will no longer assume that they should be treated the way you prefer to be treated.

Now that you are aware that your students are unique, it is time to learn more about how *you* are unique and special and how you can work successfully with each personality style.

Special Note: As you are reading the following pages, do not be concerned if you identify strongly with more than one style, even if past personality profiles labeled you with only one style. Although each person usually has one or more dominant style(s), each person is a unique blend of all four styles. There are no hard and fast rules. If you identify with more than one style, try to distinguish your top two styles, then use the tips for both styles. Also notice that some of the greatest secrets to your success will be found in the styles that you know least about. Take time to read about each of the different teaching styles and be open not only to working on building your strengths, but also to working on decreasing your struggles. The greatest teacher will be the teacher who is willing to look honestly at himself and grow, stretch and be willing to improve!

Index to Teaching Styles

If you already know your personality style, use this index to go directly to your pages.
If you do not know your personality style read through each section until it becomes clear to you as to which personality style you think you possess.

Index to Teaching Styles continued...

The High D Teacher

If you find yourself identifying with many of the following characteristics and qualities, it is very likely that this is your main style.

Strengths:

As a "**D**" teacher, you have the ability to take action. You are willing to get involved in your classroom and work hard with your students. You are an assertive person who meets life's challenges head on. You like to give your students challenging and difficult assignments. You are a determined individual, and once you make up your mind to do something, you do it. If there is a subject that you think will be too difficult for most students, you make that a personal challenge, and you find a way to teach it to your students.

As a "**D**" teacher, you have the ability to know what results you want to accomplish. If there is a lesson to be learned, then all of your students will learn it. No one in your classroom will believe that he cannot achieve the goals that you have set for him. You find a way to make everyone in your class successful.

As a "**D**" teacher, you face life. You understand that there will be obstacles to overcome in your classroom. You instill in your students the knowledge that life in general, and earning good grades in your class in particular, is tough but well worth the effort. Your persistence can be an inspiration to your students. When students try to quit, you teach them that quitting is a sign of failure, and that you will not let them fail.

As a "**D**" teacher, you can be relied upon to get the job done and to do it to the best of your ability. If papers are due to be graded and you promised them to your students, then you keep your word, no matter what the cost in effort or time.

As a "**D**" teacher, even under pressure, you will continue to do what you think is right. If that means standing up to the administration, other teachers, parents or even students, you stand firm with your beliefs. Unlike others, you ***face*** danger and difficulty. You are willing to stand alone in your decisions. You do not waver back and forth because of fear or doubt.

As a "***D***" teacher, you have confidence in your abilities. Your students, as well as others, respond to your confidence by feeling secure around you. You stand up for all students in your classroom. Ridicule and fear are not allowed. You will be a rock that your students can count on to protect them.

As a "***D***" teacher, you have natural leadership abilities. Your students look at you as the leader of the classroom. In addition, you will often be found on committees where you have the ability to take charge and make things happen for the good of the school.

As a "***D***" teacher, you have the ability to give direction to your actions. Your class will know its purpose, because you will be there leading the way, not only with your words, but more importantly, with your actions. You direct your actions toward a goal and a desired result. Your students understand that you believe that actions have specific consequences.

As a "***D***" teacher, you act with a sense of purpose. Your classroom is orderly and on task. Learning is a high priority and goofing-off is not tolerated.

As a "***D***" teacher, you have the ability to withstand hardships and rejection. You continue to push forward and search for solutions to solve problems. You are not afraid to keep going even when others would have quit under the same circumstances.

As a "***D***" teacher, you are honest and up-front with the way that you feel. Your students do not have to guess how you are feeling. You will tell them. Your students can rely on the fact that what you say is what you mean. If you feel that your students could have tried harder, you let them know. If you feel that more effort is needed or the results were not what you expected, then your students know where you stand.

As a "**D**" teacher, you have a good sense of what you can do and what your abilities are. You will not be forced into teaching something that you are not prepared to teach. You like to have a challenge, but you do not like to fail before you ever start. You believe in yourself, and you know your strengths will make a difference in others' lives. You have the ability to handle multiple assignments and complete an amazing amount of work.

What you like most about teaching:

As a "**D**" teacher, you find teaching a challenge. Every day is a new challenge just waiting to be tackled. While difficult students can frustrate some teachers, you know that with your personality you can and will handle these students. You thrive on turning average students into extraordinary students. You like choices that give you independence in the classroom. You like making decisions and having control over what information you teach.

Struggles:

You are overbearing, domineering, reckless, stubborn, overly independent, overly competitive, inflexible, arrogant, insensitive, scheming and you lack empathy. You have a one-track mind, and you never slow down and relax. You push too hard.

Each one of your strengths makes you unique, and each one of your weaknesses make you unique. As you are willing to easily recognize your strengths, so too should you be willing to work on your struggles. When you realize that your weaknesses are merely your strengths pushed to an extreme and out of control, then you can begin to get your struggles under control.

*Let's look at how a "**D**" teacher would handle each one of the four different personalities in the classroom.*

The D Teaching Style and the... D Student

Strengths:

As long as you and your student share the same desires and direction, you will experience harmony. Together you will be able to accomplish a lot as a team. Your mutual goals, admiration and desire to get results can be very positive and affirming to the "***D***" student. You give these students a challenge, and they respond. You draw strength from this type of motivated student.

Struggles:

Power struggles over control are the most frequent source of friction and fighting. A simple misunderstanding can turn into a war. Since both you and your "***D***" student are competitive, you both want to win every battle, no matter the cost. Neither of you will want to give in or give up. You think if you give an inch, this student will take a mile, and in many cases, you're right. But if you cannot reach a compromise through choices, then your classroom can become a battleground.

Strategies:

- When working with "***D***" students, don't force issues with them.
- Talk straight and to the point. Don't threaten or give ultimatums.
- Balance holding a hard line with allowing "***D***" students to have some areas over which they can have control. Whenever possible, give the "***D***" students choices.
- Do not give lectures to "***D***" students. When possible, give direct, one-word or two-word commands. For example, "Sarah, sit down! Johnny, be quiet!"

- Discuss with your "***D***" students the areas of greatest disruption. Sit down with them, one on one, and give them some working rules and stick to them. This trains the "***D***" students to become more responsible and to understand limits.
- Don't argue with "***D***" students. If you do, they have won the battle, because they were able to control your emotions and reactions.

Helpful sentences for "*D*" students (and their parents):

- "You are a determined student."
- "You are up front with people."
- "You have confidence in yourself and your abilities."
- "You have a strong will."

The D Teaching Style and the... I Student

Strengths:

Both of you are confident and enjoy a fast-paced approach to life. Your student will want to please you so desperately that he will follow (or at least appear to follow) your leadership. Because you are the leader, you will be able to control and teach this student much about self-discipline. Your "***I***" student will also appreciate your desire to set goals and stick to them.

Struggles:

Your desire to accomplish goals and get results can easily be frustrated by the "take-life-as-it-comes" attitude of the "***I***" student. Frequent conflicts may occur when your focus on getting things done clashes with the "***I***" student's focus on having fun and talking with his friends. The "***I***" student will have a difficult time adapting to your goal of giving you short and to the point answers. Also, the "***I***" student's tendency toward disorganization and not completing tasks can cause you to become angry.

Strategies:

- Realize that "***I***" students may never have your focus or your goal-orientation, but that does not make them a bad person.
- Make class as fun as possible.
- Be ready to modify your need for a totally structured environment.
- Provide ideas for transforming talk into action
- Write down the details of what you expect. Keep rules simple and easy to follow.

- Listen enthusiastically to your "***I***" student's long stories and tales. This skill of your "***I***" student is to be encouraged.
- Give a lot of praise, affection and approval.
- Accept the feelings and emotions of your "***I***" students as well as their insistence on facts.
- Your strength to stand firm and alone under pressure can provide an excellent role model for this student whose greatest struggle tends to be succumbing to peer pressure.

Helpful sentences for "*I*" students (and their parents):

- "You are an outgoing student."
- "You are a persuasive student."
- "You have a lot of enthusiasm. It is contagious."
- "You are very gifted in expressing your thoughts."

Strengths:

You like to lead, and this student likes to follow. He will feel secure with you as long as you show controlled, stable behavior. You have the ability to create an environment where this student feels very safe from ridicule from other students. The "**S**" student appreciates your ability to keep a commitment.

Struggles:

If you come on too strong, this student will be easily intimidated and will take it personally. Also, hard charging "**D**" teachers often misunderstand the easygoing "**S**" student and mislabel them as "weak." Although confrontation and a fast pace come easily for you, this puts undo stress on your "**S**" student. This can easily lead to self-esteem problems for the "**S**" student. Do not yell or be harsh with the "**S**" student. He will shut down in your class if you overpower him.

Strategies:

- Do not expect the "**S**" student to figure out how to accomplish a task. Spell it out, step-by-step, exactly what to do.
- They want to please you, so they want to know how you want something done.
- Watch how you say things. The "**S**" student is very sensitive and can easily be hurt by spontaneous, off-the-cuff, negative comments and anger.
- Do not push them into heated competition.

- Even though you feel that it will motivate them, never compare the "***S***" student to anyone else. This is demoralizing for them and can cause them to give up trying.
- "***S***" students need to feel close to their teachers. As difficult as it sounds, to give your students a sense of belonging and acceptance, you must make a special effort to spend time with the "***S***" students and give them plenty of affection.
- Remember that it typically makes "***S***" students uncomfortable to stand in front of a class. They are even uncomfortable when they are called on to answer questions during class.

Helpful sentences for "*S*" students (and their parents):

- "You have the ability to form deep, lasting friendships."
- "You give others the benefit of the doubt."
- "You are a caring student."
- "You don't seem pressured by time."

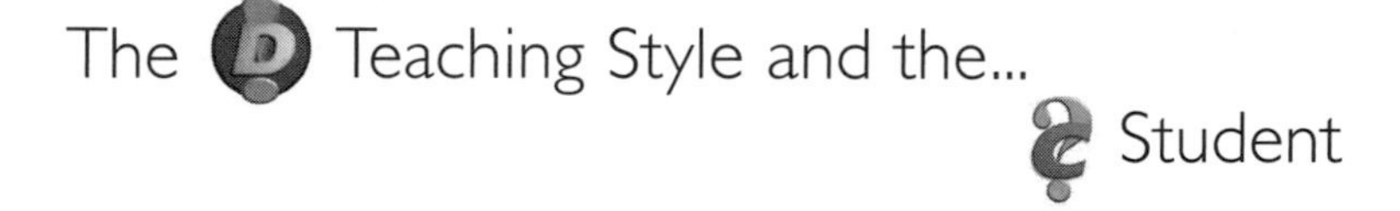

The D Teaching Style and the... C Student

Strengths:

Since both of you focus on tasks and enjoy working independently, you share some common ground. As a team, with your direction and the student's attention to detail, you can accomplish a lot. Both of you are very task-oriented. This is a great similarity and will serve you well with the "**C**" student. The "**C**" student appreciates your ability to move forward and make a decision.

Struggles:

You tend to jump into a project quickly, whereas the "**C**" student likes to think things through in detail. Remember that your "**C**" students have a difficult time with brevity. They like to give you all the facts which will, in turn, try your patience and create conflict. You both want results, but the student wants things done right, and you want things done now. This difference in pace is a chief source of conflict. Also, your tendency to control things can be discouraging to this student who does not want to feel pressured.

Strategies:

- DO NOT become impatient with "**C**" students.
- Don't rush or push them. Give them time to make decisions.
- Allow "**C**" students time to gather all the facts and do things "correctly" as they define "correct."
- Be careful with criticism. While criticism may motivate you, "**C**" students may deeply internalize criticism, and it may seriously damage their self-esteem.

- Callous comments or acts of aggression will immobilize "**C**" students.
- Be prepared to answer the student's **WHY** questions, and patiently provide in-depth explanations. If you move on without answering their questions, you may lose their respect.
- "**C**" students need you to give quality answers to their questions, not just "because" or "I told you so" answers.
- Accept and affirm their cautious nature. Do not expect them to be a risk-taker like you.
- Listen to your "**C**" students.
- The reasons they do what they do are usually thought out thoroughly.

Helpful sentences for "C" students (and their parents):

- "You tend to be a quiet student."
- "You enjoy spending time by yourself."
- "You have high standards."
- "You are interested in key facts and information."

The High I Teacher

If you find yourself identifying with many of the following characteristics and qualities, it is very likely that this is your main style.

Strengths:

As an "*I*" teacher, you are a people person. You like your students, and you want them to like you. You want your students to accept you for who are - a great big ball of excitement and energy! When you are in the front of your class, you know it's time to perform. Your motto is definitely "There's no business like show business." You have the ability to make your students feel at ease. You take the toughest students and build bridges to them with your laughter.

As an "*I*" teacher, you are a gifted communicator. You never have to worry about what you are going to say. You have the great ability to express your thoughts, opinions, beliefs and ideas through stories. Your lessons are unique and exciting. Your communication skills help you pass on to your students the ideas you think are worthwhile.

As an "*I*" teacher, you are a great cheerleader for your students. You are not in front of them or behind them but right beside them, inspiring them all of the way. You have a talent for lifting the spirits of your students. When your students have had a hard day, you have the ability to forget about yourself and your problems and help your students see that things really can work out for the best. You are the ultimate encourager.

As an "*I*" teacher, you have a gift for talking, so that your students clearly understand what you are saying. When you talk, your students listen with their imaginations. Not only is your way of speaking expressive, but you also like to use your hands to make a point. You will also use great facial expressions as well as intense emotion and tone of voice to drive home key points. Your expressive style enables your students to see life much more fully.

As an "***I***" teacher, you have the ability to look on the lighter side of life, and you find humor to share with your students. If there is a key event in the world, you can find the humor in it and share that with your students. You are so much fun to be around that your students respond to you by wanting to talk to you before and after class. Your humor also helps your students relax, especially if they are under pressure.

As an "***I***" teacher, you have a creative and active imagination. You can turn the most boring lesson into a full opera, play or concert. Your ability to create is also a great help to other teachers who are looking for new and innovative teaching lessons and techniques. Although all teachers can't be as lively as you, they can still benefit from your great imagination and creativity.

As an "***I***" teacher, you pour yourself into your activities. You live life with a passion and at a fast pace. You like the fact that when the door closes to your classroom, you can, with enthusiasm, make a difference in your students' lives. You make a great impact on your students. You help them feel more positive about school and themselves.

As an "***I***" teacher, you have the ability to influence students, so that your students will agree with you. This special gift can be easily abused. If you tell your students that vitamins are essential for them, they will take vitamins. Your gift of persuasion enables you to achieve leadership positions. You can be found on many committees, and you are always involved with your school.

As an "***I***" teacher, you look for the best in all of your students and in all situations. You have a hopeful, positive attitude, even when things don't look promising. If your students are struggling with an assignment or with material that you are covering, you remain positive and work to remedy the situation. You have the ability to inspire your students to do their best, instead of settling for mediocrity.

As an "*I*" teacher, you are upbeat and flexible. Whereas other teachers might need to plan, you can simply jump at a moment's notice and be spontaneous. You are very rarely disturbed by changes in the classroom. In fact, you are at your best when you can react to a new and ever-changing environment. You are a unique and special teacher.

What you like most about teaching:

As an "*I*" teacher, you find teaching exciting and fun. Every day is a new adventure just waiting for you to explore. You love teaching, because you get to be the star for each one of your students. Besides being the star of your classroom, you love teaching because of the laughter and admiration that your students feed you when you are performing. You thrive on turning average students into extraordinary students through inspiration. You love making your students laugh. You draw great strength from knowing that you have their approval.

Struggles:

You are overly dependent on what others think and say about you. You give in easily to peer pressure, overcommit yourself, talk too much, interrupt while others are talking, give insincere compliments, tend to exaggerate, use humor to ignore problems and find yourself never being serious. You are disorganized, overbearing, unrealistic, overly emotional and impulsive. You are a daydreamer, a smooth talker and a poor listener.

Each one of your strengths makes you unique, and each one of your weaknesses make you unique. As you are willing to easily recognize your strengths, so too should you be willing to work on your struggles. When you realize that your weaknesses are merely your strengths pushed to an extreme and out of control, then you can begin to get your struggles under control.

*Let's look at how an "**I**" teacher would handle each one of the four different personalities in the classroom.*

The I Teaching Style and the... D Student

Strengths:

As an "***I***" teacher, you will delight in the strengths of your "***D***" student. You will brag about his accomplishments and share the spotlight in any honors. Both of you possess confident, activity-driven outlooks on life, and both of you want to look like winners. Your frequent praise for achievement along with your encouragement is motivating to the "***D***" student, who desires to be admired. The "***D***" will appreciate your ability to stay relaxed and have fun. The "***D***" student will also appreciate your ability to easily build relationships.

Struggles:

Because you want to be liked by your students, you have a tendency to become too permissive. Your "***D***" students may seem confrontational when they think that you are not looking for results. While "***D***" students need some freedom and choices, they must also have well-defined and firm boundaries. If the "***I***" teacher is not careful, the "***D***" student will take control of the classroom.

Strategies:

- Set clearly defined limits and boundaries and stick to them.
- When rules are broken and lines are crossed, you must follow through with previously determined consequences and discipline. The "***D***" student tends to take advantage of any inconsistency or lack of follow-through on your part. They are determined to take over whenever possible.

- Do not be afraid of confrontation. Expect it.
- When correcting, be brief and to the point.
- "***D***" students do not want or need long-winded explanations.
- Give them one-word or two-word commands, and expect them to obey.
- Realize that these students will frequently push you out of your comfort zone. This may be emotionally draining for you.

Helpful sentences for "*D*" students (and their parents):

- "You have strong ideas about things."
- "You aren't easily pushed off task."
- "You have drive."
- "You like to get results from your efforts."

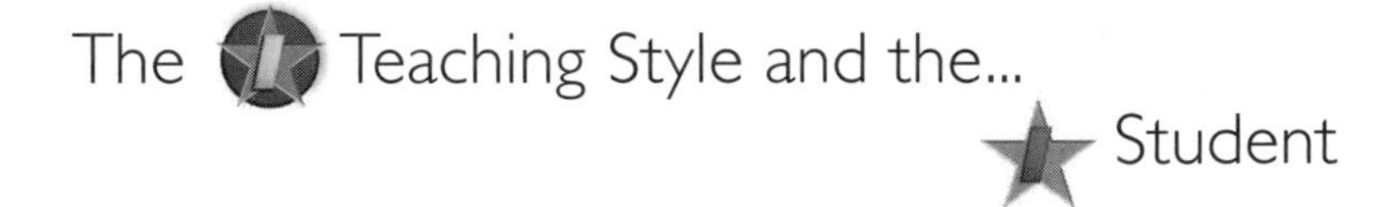

The I Teaching Style and the... I Student

Strengths:

You and your "***I***" students live life enthusiastically and optimistically. You both enjoy being with people, and you both like to have fun. Both of you want to impress others, and you freely give compliments and praise. In fact, you can become a cheerleader to each other. When you make mistakes, you both will give a lot of slack and tend to forgive easily. Expect your "***I***" students, because of your outgoing nature and attitude, to really open up with you and the class.

Struggles:

Because both teacher and student tend to live life emotionally, you may end up competing to be the center of attention. Do not be offended by high "***I***" students who try to upstage you, because they will try. Also, because of your nature, you will invite long stories from your "***I***" students. Do not steal their thunder by competing against them for attention. However, because you are not as strict as you could be, be aware that these students are really going to push your buttons.

Strategies:

- Remember to listen to your "***I***" students. They like to talk as much as you do.
- Realize that your tendency to be overly permissive may help produce an even greater lack of responsibility in this student.
- Learn to incorporate some of the strengths of both the "***D***" and the "***C***" teaching styles in order to give balance

to your natural teaching style - especially the control of the "***D***" and the cautious, calculating nature of the "***C***".

- Realize that this student dislikes details as much as you dislike details.
- When covering important information, make sure you repeat it, and that you have it written down for the "***I***" student.
- Set limits and boundaries. Follow through with discipline.
- Resist bailing out "***I***" students when they fail to follow through with an assignment or don't do their homework. Resisting the impulse to rescue them will not be easy, but it is necessary in order for "***I***" students to grow into competent, responsible adults.

Helpful sentences for "*I*" students (and their parents):

- "You like positive friendships."
- "You have a great sense of humor."
- "You are a great storyteller."
- "You are gifted at expressing your thoughts and opinions."

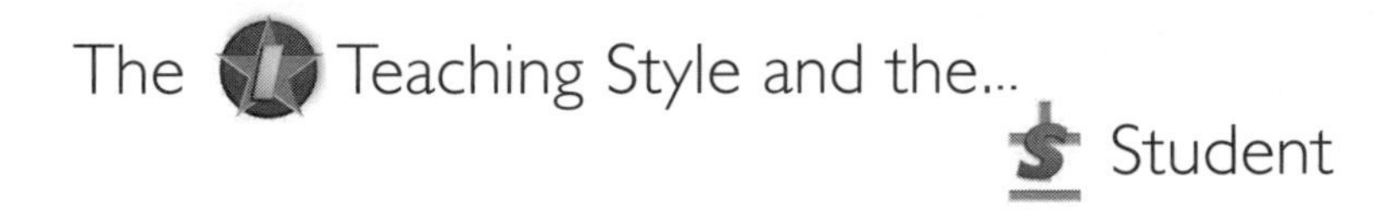

The "I" Teaching Style and the... "S" Student

Strengths:

An interactive "***I***" teacher will appreciate the easygoing, relaxed nature of the "***S***" student. An "***I***" teacher likes to talk, and the "***S***" student enjoys listening. These two styles tend to get along very well together.

Struggles:

Ironically, most struggles between "***I***" teachers and "***S***" students center around differences in pace. The high "***I***" teacher enjoys a fast-paced, exciting environment, and this is exactly what the high "***S***" student wants to avoid. The high "***I***" likes noise and confusion; the high "***S***" desires quiet. The high "***I***" teacher thrives on spontaneity, variety and quick changes. The high "***S***" student is slow to change, enjoys routines and dislikes surprises and unplanned changes.

Strategies:

- Although it is very difficult to completely slow down, try to have intervals of slower times for your "***S***" students.
- Let your "***S***" students respond at their own slower pace without trying to fill in their questions, comments or answers for them.
- Allow your "***S***" students time to make decisions.
- Tone down your enthusiasm.
- Don't embarrass your "***S***" students by being overly enthusiastic about their achievements in front of other students. Provide support and encouragement in private rather than in front of the class.

- Be sincere in your praise and appreciation of your "***S***" students without being fake.
- Accept their shyness and the fact that they may be slow to warm up to new people and events, especially you and your classroom.
- Whenever possible, give your "***S***" students advance warning as to what and how things may change.
- If there are going to be changes in the teaching material, for example, if you are going to remove or add material on a test, then do not surprise them. Simply tell them ahead of time.
- Ask more questions, and then listen carefully to your "***S***" students' answers.
- Ask for their help in getting tasks accomplished. "***S***" students love to feel that their contributions are valued and wanted.
- Remember that it typically makes "***S***" students uncomfortable to stand in front of a class. They are even uncomfortable when they are called on to answer questions during class.

Helpful sentences for "*S*" students (and their parents):

- "You are an accepting person."
- "You feel for others when they are hurt or under stress."
- "You are trusting of others."
- "You have a calming influence on others."

The I Teaching Style and the... C Student

Strengths:

You can learn much from each other as the strengths of one provide a good balance to the weaknesses of the other. With your help, your "**C**" student can learn not to take things so seriously and have more fun. And, as an "***I***" teacher, your "**C**" students can help you think things through in a more analytical way.

Struggles:

Your differences can lead to frequent misunderstandings. You love to talk and tell stories, but sometimes your "**C**" students need you to give more details and fewer stories. Also, because you are so verbal, you may not notice the indirect way of sharing concerns that typically come from the "**C**" type.

Strategies:

- Listen to your "**C**" students so that you will better understand them.
- Be alert to subtle nuances in what "**C**" students say. They use words sparingly, and each word has meaning.
- Tone down your emotional reactions and your enthusiasm.
- Be more factual and objective - especially in the midst of conflict.
- Realize that these students have a drive for perfection that is as deeply felt as your need for fun. They cannot simply "lighten up" and "laugh off" mistakes.
- Allow your "**C**" students time alone to be disappointed when their work doesn't measure up to their standards.

- Don't rush or push them.
- Allow them time alone to do quality work.
- Be sincere in your praise and appreciation of their work.
- Tell them what they did well in specific descriptive terms, rather than simply saying "Great job!" "Terrific!" or "You did a fantastic job!"
- Your "**C**" students' worst fear is criticism of their work. Be gentle when correcting.
- Never call out their grades in front of the classroom without their permission, even if they are good.
- Don't expect them to take risks. Accept their cautious nature.

Helpful sentences for "C" students (and their parents):

- "You always do your best work."
- "You are a person who believes in doing things right."
- "You have the ability to think things through."
- "You have a questioning mind."

The High S Teacher

If you find yourself identifying with many of the following characteristics and qualities, it is very likely that this is your main style.

Strengths:

As an "**S**" teacher, you enjoy building relationships. You try to notice things that interest your students. You notice whether they play sports, read, perform drama or just like working on a computer. "**S**" type teachers usually talk to students about these things, and you take a genuine interest in their lives. You make it a priority to point out books and special events in which you know they would be interested.

As an "**S**" teacher, you have a keen ability to focus on and listen to your students. You not only listen to their words, but you also read their body language and sense how they feel. You listen so well that you hear what others sometimes miss. You have the ability to make students feel special, and you will find that your students are willing to express their feelings to you without feeling threatened. In a word, you make your students feel safe.

As an "**S**" teacher, you are able to create a routine for your students. Your ability to create a steady, serene and loving environment benefits your students. Your students know what to expect, and they respect you for this trait.

As an "**S**" teacher, in the beginning of your career, you might think that you are not experienced enough to be a valuable part of the faculty. However, as you mature, you realize that you no longer just think about yourself and your abilities, but you look at the whole educational team as one working unit. You are willing to do your part to help the team succeed. When other teachers need your help with projects, you are ready to help. You enjoy working together with others to accomplish tasks. As a high "**S**" you often hold back and keep valuable insights to yourself, because you sometimes may feel that what you have to say is not important. However, the truth is that you and your ideas are a valuable and necessary part of the success and progress of your team and your school.

As an "**S**" teacher, people admire your dependability. You can be counted on to fulfill your duties. If lessons plans are due on Friday, then they are ready on Friday. If you have a specific duty to do, you do it.

As an "**S**" teacher, you go by the rules. Whatever the rules are, you can be found following them. You like boundaries and guidelines to follow. It helps you to be told how to do things or how someone wants a specific task to be completed. You appreciate instructions that are written down for you. "**S**" type personalities like to follow easy instructions, and they generally look for ways to simplify tasks. If parents ask you to try a specific approach with their child, you are more than willing to try it for the benefit of the student.

As an "**S**" teacher, you are easygoing. Moreover, you have the ability to take the emphasis off yourself and direct it toward other teachers, or most importantly, on your students. You do not want nor need anyone looking at you.

As an "**S**" teacher, although you do not enjoy the limelight and you don't talk that much, people that know you realize that when you do talk, you are saying something of great value. Therefore, people listen to you. You are a unique and special teacher.

What you like most about teaching:

As an "***S***" teacher, you find teaching rewarding, because you can see that others are benefiting from your abilities. Every day there is a new student that you can love. You love the appreciation your students show you. You thrive on turning average students into extraordinary students through your kindness and appreciation.

Struggles:

You are lazy, unmotivated, overly accommodating, a pushover, easily influenced, weak-willed, non-communicative, inflexible, stubborn and too lenient. You resist change, and you resist compliments from others. You discount your own ability, and others easily take advantage of you. You give in too easily. You lack initiative and assertiveness.

Each one of your strengths makes you unique, and each one of your weaknesses make you unique. As you are willing to easily recognize your strengths, so too should you be willing to work on your struggles. When you realize that your weaknesses are merely your strengths pushed to an extreme and out of control, then you can begin to get your struggles under control.

*Let's look at how an "**S**" teacher would handle each one of the four different personalities in the classroom.*

The  Teaching Style and the... Student

Strengths:
An "***S***" teacher has the ability to provide the encouragement on which "***D***" students thrive as they seek to achieve their goals and exert leadership.

Struggles:
Since "***D***" students desire constant control and instant action, they can easily exhaust an "***S***" teacher like you, who wants things to stay calm and peaceful. The biggest problem with this combination comes in the area of discipline. You tend to be too lenient. You want to avoid conflict, and they know it. They can easily take advantage of you. You want peace at all costs, and the long-term result can be an uncontrollable student.

Strategies:
- "***D***" students need some areas over which they have control. Just make sure you are not controlled by them, and don't become disheartened when they don't need you for some activity.
- They like to do things themselves. Don't take it personally.
- Make strong statements and establish your authority.
- Force yourself to take a stand.
- Be decisive and stick to your decisions.
- Realize that you will be tested. It's important that you do not waver.
- Understand that being more direct will not be easy for you, but it is necessary.
- Don't feel you are a failure, because your "***D***" students are so different from you. They are the way they are because of their design.

Helpful sentences for "*D*" students (and their parents):
- "You say exactly what you think."
- "You set your mind on a goal and go for it."
- "You play hard. You play to win."
- "You can make a decision without others' input."

The S Teaching Style and the... I Student

Strengths:
You have the potential to get along well. An "***S***" teacher loves to have a good time, and the "***I***" student can provide the entertainment. Both you and your student provide the praise and appreciation which each of you needs to feel good about yourselves.

Struggles:
Keeping up with the pace of this student can be a challenge for you. Your "***I***" student likes change, and he moves from activity to activity, like a tornado.

Strategies:
- You must be firm and set limits with these students. Their persuasive, fast-talking ability can leave you speechless and wondering why you gave permission for some activity.
- Don't overdo for these students. They tend to dislike work and will let you do everything for them if you are not careful. This can breed irresponsibility into the students. You do not want them to go through life thinking someone else will take care of them, so they can coast along and have fun.
- Don't bail your "***I***" students out when they have not been responsible with homework or keeping on a schedule. Let them experience the logical consequences of being disorganized or forgetful.
- Help them become more organized by writing down how something is to be done in a step-by-step manner.
- Give them tips on how to make a "to do" list, but don't be surprised when this student frequently loses the list.

Helpful sentences for "*I*" students (and their parents):
- "You notice everything going on around you."
- "You eagerly participate in many activities."
- "You share your thoughts and opinions easily."
- "You easily motivate others."

Strengths:
You have a lot in common and can easily enjoy being with each other. Both of you appreciate a relaxed, calm, peaceful atmosphere and work to keep things that way. You both help each other.

Struggles:
The biggest trouble comes in the area of communication. You both talk indirectly. You both will suggest things, but neither of you will want to make decisions. Also, neither of you wants to initiate anything that might result in change. If you are too accommodating, the "***S***" student may become too dependent upon you. Also, since neither of you wants to upset the other, hurt feelings can be suppressed. Over time this unwillingness to bring up unpleasant issues can become a problem.

Strategies:
- Balance doing things for your "***S***" students while encouraging them to do things for themselves.
- Initiate more and be more decisive.
- Realize that some conflict and change is healthy.
- Life changes constantly, so don't overprotect your "***S***" students from this reality.
- Draw out how your "***S***" students feel and honestly share how you feel.
- Don't sweep hurt or negative feelings under the rug, hoping they will go away.

Helpful sentences for "*S*" students (and their parents):
- "You like to watch before participating."
- "You like to check things out before you make a decision."
- "You are a sensitive person."
- "You don't like conflict."

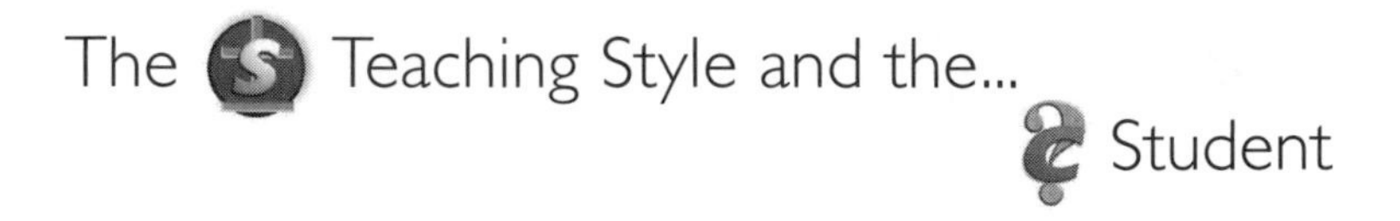

The S Teaching Style and the... C Student

Strengths:

This combination generally works extremely well together. Both of you tend to be slower paced. Neither of you are pushy. You both prefer to avoid conflict. You can enjoy the "**C**" student in your classroom without a lot of conversation.

Struggles:

In this combination, the critical nature of your student can easily result in hurt feelings on your part. You have the tendency to suppress hard feelings rather than talk about them. The student's inner, intuitive, logical approach to life can at times clash with your more feelings-oriented focus. Also, since you naturally work to develop close relationships, you may feel concern about the cool, calculated manner of these students.

Strategies:

- Recognize these students need privacy.
- If there is a conflict, give them time alone to think before discussing it.
- They need private time to recharge after stress. Do not interpret this as rejection.
- Don't push your "**C**" students into closeness.
- Choose your sharing time carefully. Talk about how you feel. Then listen for understanding if you sense the student has withdrawn and shut down.
- Be prepared to give in-depth explanations in a patient manner.

- Allow them time for disappointment when they have not met their own high standards - especially after receiving grades.
- Give sincere, descriptive praise and show appreciation for their work.
- Don't overreact to their tendency to be critical, but gently guide them to accept shortcomings in themselves and in others.

Helpful sentences for "*C*" students (and their parents):

- "You like things to be just right."
- "You think deeply about things."
- "You like things to be organized."
- "You do things precisely and accurately."

The High C Teacher

If you find yourself identifying with many of the following characteristics and qualities, it is very likely that this is your main style.

Strengths:

As a "**C**" teacher, you have the ability to see the strengths and weaknesses of your students. You quickly notice your students' possible problem areas. When something is not working, you will investigate different strategies to help each student succeed.

As a "**C**" teacher, you have the ability to look beneath the surface of everyday problems, conflicts and situations. You have the ability to carefully weigh all relevant aspects of a problem. You think ahead and look at possible scenarios that might arise and, through cautious and detailed planning, you eliminate foreseeable problems. You are able to see and understand all viewpoints, even those that differ from your own. You can readily point out solutions to others in a logical way.

As a "**C**" teacher, you are a valuable person on any planning committee. While others might give great ideas, you have the ability to look at all of the variables and foresee possible problems. With this skill, you save others valuable time, money and effort. Your motto could be "Assume the worst, so things turn out for the best."

As a "**C**" teacher, you explore and experiment with new technology that your school will be implementing. You like time to work with new technology and practice with it before you ever use it in your classroom.

As a "**C**" teacher, your lesson plans are complete and well prepared. Your papers are run off, and your supplies are ready and waiting. Your classroom is neat and orderly. Everything is in its place, and everything has a place. Very little time, if any, is wasted in searching for materials.

As a "**C**" teacher, you have the ability to take on projects or say *no* to projects, depending on the perceived value to you and your students. If you feel that your class will benefit, then you are more likely to agree to the project.

As a "**C**" teacher, you work hard and strive for excellence in all that you do. Your students can count on you to know the in-depth, factual meaning of what they are studying. In addition, your students know what your expectations are, both in and out of the classroom. Your students know that rules are important to you, and that you expect them to follow the rules.

As a "**C**" teacher, you will go above and beyond the call of duty. You far exceed minimum expectations. If the state requires a percentage of passing students, then you will want to have everyone in your classroom reaching the expectations. You try to instill your desire for excellence in your students.

As a "**C**" teacher, your standards of excellence are very important to you. You do not settle for less in yourself or your students. Your motto can be "Careless mistakes are for the careless." You take pride in all aspects of your profession, from the preparation of assignments to the success of your students.

What you like most about teaching:

As a "**C**" teacher, you find teaching rewarding. Every day is a new task to complete. You thrive on turning average students into extraordinary students by a systematic approach of facts. You thoroughly enjoy researching and presenting what you have learned and mastered.

Struggles:

You are overly critical, overly analytical, unsociable, nosy, distrustful, insensitive, unfeeling, rigid, picky and you have a lack of emotional responses. You ask too many questions, and you take too much time completing tasks. You are a perfectionist, and you worry too much. In addition, it can be hard to follow your logic.

Each one of your strengths makes you unique, and each one of your weaknesses make you unique. As you are willing to easily recognize your strengths, so too should you be willing to work on your struggles. When you realize that your weaknesses are merely your strengths pushed to an extreme and out of control, then you can begin to get your struggles under control.

*Let's look at how a "**C**" teacher would handle each one of the four different personalities in the classroom.*

The C Teaching Style and the... D Student

Strengths:

Both teacher and student share a similar bent toward accomplishing tasks. As long as they share these goals, they can be mutually helpful and very effective as a pair.

Struggles:

If teacher and student have opposing goals, the "***C***" teacher will find himself in a hopeless battle. The "***C***" teacher wants things done "right," according to his standards. But "right" to a "***D***" is seldom as complicated as the "***C***" seems to make it. "***D***" students simply wants to do it their way and get it done. "***D***" students will tend to make decisions and do things quickly, missing key details that are important to the "***C***" teacher.

Strategies:

- Give your "***D***" students some responsibility, and keep yourself from stepping in to try to make things better. They need to be in charge of something.
- Be lavish in affirming the goals and accomplishments of your "***D***" students. This may not come naturally for you since you often see how something can be done just a little bit better.
- Recognize that taking risks is important to "***D***" students. Set limits according to wisdom and safety.
- Accept that life with a "***D***" student will be one change and challenge after another.
- Recognize that "***D***" students need physical activity.
- Try not to argue with them; your reasoning may not be convincing.

- Most of all, don't expect perfection.
- Be cautious about setting your standards so high that your "***D***" students feel that they will never be able to reach them. Even a "***D***" will quit trying if he is constantly criticized for not measuring up to your standards.

Helpful sentences for "*D*" students (and their parents):
- "You are committed and decisive."
- "You are assertive."
- "You are independent and capable."
- "You are quick to respond to new situations."

Strengths:
Your love for details and doing things right is exactly what this student needs to be more balanced and successful in life. Your "*I*" student can be a source of freshness and joy to you, because you tend to be serious.

Struggles:
You like things at a slower pace, while your "*I*" students like a faster pace. You may find it difficult to understand that these students have a persistent, intense need for fun. Because of your high standards, the "*I*" students may not receive the praise and recognition that they need.

Strategies:
- You must modify your expectations for the "*I*" students.
- Realize that they will never give the same attention to details that you do.
- Be aware that the "*I*" students have a hunger for acceptance and approval. Look for strengths and praise them at every opportunity.
- Enjoy your "*I*" students for who they are, even though their strengths may be different from yours.
- Stop working on your projects and tasks long enough to give your "*I*" students your focused attention.
- Listen enthusiastically to their stories and tales. It energizes them to talk and have you listen attentively.
- Most of all, don't push for perfection. Don't set your standards so high that your "*I*" students feel that they will never reach them.

Helpful sentences for "*I*" students (and their parents):
- "You are flexible."
- "You are full of surprises."
- "You are full of energy."
- "You really enjoy being with others."

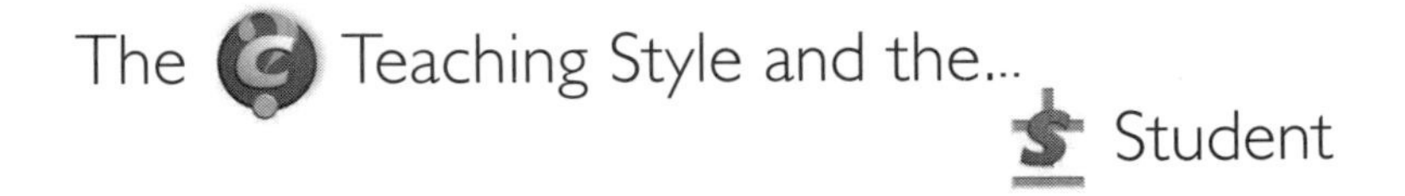

The C Teaching Style and the... S Student

Strengths:

Both the "**C**" teacher and the "**S**" student take things slowly so you both enjoy a more reserved, low-key relationship. The "**C**" teacher will appreciate the "**S**" student's easygoing, agreeable nature.

Struggles:

You may be frustrated when the "**S**" student doesn't think through things the way you do or share your enthusiasm for key details. You also may worry about why you cannot seem to motivate this student to strive for the same standards of excellence by which you operate.

Strategies:

- Be aware of your tendency to focus on critical tasks and to do things correctly.
- Balance your interaction by exploring how your "**S**" students feel and what is going on in their world.
- Be more open and share your feelings with your "**S**" students.
- Draw "**S**" students out with appreciation.
- Take time to explain how you want something done. Do not expect your "**S**" students to figure out all the details by themselves.
- Show sincere appreciation for any effort, even if it does not come up to your standards.
- Be careful with your criticism. Criticism can sound harsh even if you don't intend it to be.
- Most important of all, don't set your standards so high that your "**S**" students feel that they will never be able to live up to them. If you do, the "**S**" students will feel inadequate and not valued, and they will simply give up.

Helpful sentences for "S" students (and their parents):

- "You don't rush into decisions."
- "You are a good listener."
- "You are compassionate and tenderhearted."
- "You always follow through."

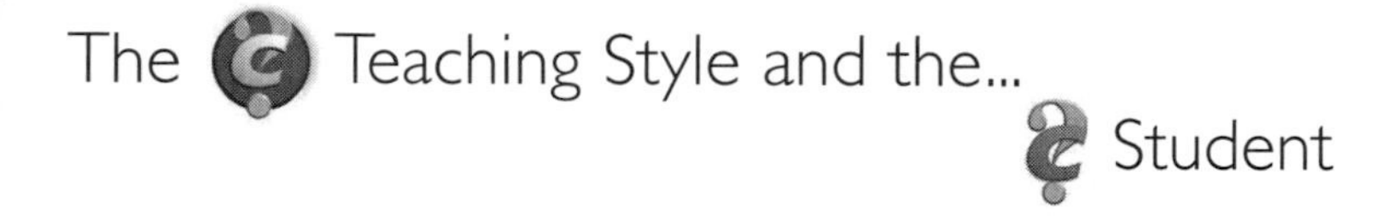

The C Teaching Style and the... C Student

Strengths:

This is a natural combination to produce a student prodigy. You can enjoy working hard together on some task or project and give full attention to what needs to be done. You both are prone to seriousness. Both teacher and student are dedicated to quality, excellence and doing things the right way.

Struggles:

The trouble comes when you and your "**C**" student disagree on whose way is the "right" way. Both of you can quickly shut down and withdraw to plan your next move. Both of you tend to wage a war of indirect communication.

Strategies:

- Be open when your "**C**" students suggest a different way of doing something.
- Be willing to be flexible on some of your standards in order to finish a job in a mutually acceptable way.
- Be careful when you correct your "**C**" students. You know that criticism of your work is one of your greatest fears.
- Don't overreact when your "**C**" students criticize you.
- Show plenty of affection and emotion. Like you, this student needs to feel loved and valued. They may not be naturally affectionate.
- Most of all, don't set your standards so high that your "**C**" students feel that they will never be able to reach them.

Helpful sentences for "C" students (and their parents):

- "You like things done in a logical way."
- "You are a good evaluator."
- "You are a serious person."
- "You like to understand all you can before you make a decision."

Final Food for Thought....

In the general population, the percentages of the four personality styles are as follows:

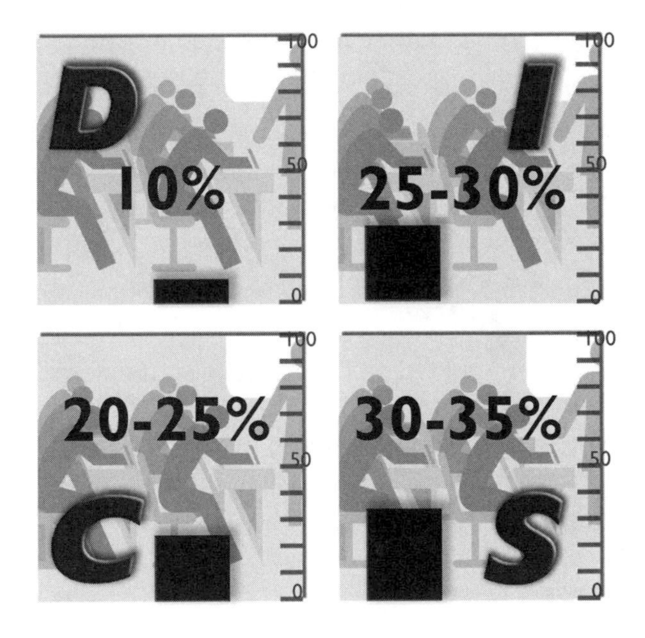

It's time to make you really want to use this information! As you read the following information, ask yourself:

Is it important to adapt and adjust my teaching style to meet the needs of all of my students?

If you are a "***D***" teacher and only use your "***D***" qualities to teach, you will successfully teach 10% of your class, leaving behind 90% of your students.

If you are an "***I***" teacher and use only your "***I***" qualities to teach, you will successfully teach 25-30% of your class, leaving behind 70-75% of your students.

If you are an "***S***" teacher and use only your "***S***" qualities to teach, you will successfully teach 30-35% of your class, leaving behind 65-70% of your students.

If you are a "***C***" teacher and use only your "***C***" qualities to teach, you will successfully teach 20-25% of your class, leaving behind 75-80% of your students.

Suppose we take the best case scenario. That would be a teacher who has an "***S / C***" blend. Then we add the combined percentages of the "***S***" (35%) and the "***C***"(25%). That teacher would only successfully teach 60% of the class, leaving behind 40% of the students. Unfortunately, the students left behind are the "**D**s" and "***I***s" who relate very little to that natural teaching style. If you are wondering, these same students are the ones who would consistently give you the most problems.

So before you decide whether or not to use this information, think about the positive impact you can have on all of your students if you do.

Go for it! *You can do it!* You are a unique and special teacher!

Parenting Section

The Dominant/Directing Parent :

Natural Strengths:
Goal-oriented and decisive actions
Natural Limitations:
Impatient and blunt
Pushed to an extreme, the dominant parent may become autocratic or dictatorial.

High "***D***" parents like to get immediate results when they ask their children to do something. They like challenges and choices in life, They may stir up a little excitement if things become too routine or relaxed.

- They fear that others will take advantage of them.
- They speak directly and sometimes bluntly. They like others to "get to the point quickly" in sharing a request or telling a story. They do not like dealing with other people's emotions.
- They seek to maintain control. They like doing things on their terms and may use fear to gain respect.

High "*D*" parents can work to keep their strengths from becoming limitations by...

- Accepting that they will not be in charge all the time.
- Listening more, being careful not to give answers too quickly, explaining more, developing sensitivity to family members' feelings, verbalizing positive emotions

and allowing others to ask questions and share their feelings.
- Resisting the impulse to become impatient with slower performance.
- Openly admitting when they've made mistakes.
- Pacing themselves and making sure that there are family fun times when everybody (including the High "***D***" parent) can relax.

The Influencing/Interacting Parent

Natural Strengths:
Fun-loving and optimistic
Natural Limitations:
Disorganized and not detail-oriented
Pushed to an extreme, the interacting parent can become too permissive.

- High "***I***" parents love to gather their friends and their children together and talk, talk, talk. They love story-telling and wrestling. Of all parents, they are the most free to play with their children. They enjoy outward displays of affection.
- They fear loss of approval and may avoid disciplining their children in order to stay liked. They tend to be permissive parents, because it isn't fun to be consistent in raising children.
- They tend to speak emotionally. They speak more aggressively than they will act. They have a tendency to exaggerate.
- They seek to maintain a friendly, upbeat home life.

High "*I*" parents can keep their strengths from becoming limitations by...
- Being more organized, so that they do not neglect what

is really important – their family. They need to write down significant dates and events.
- Watching out that in their excitement to tell stories, they do not exaggerate to the point of not being entirely honest.
- Guarding against allowing their fear of not being liked to keep them from appropriate discipline.

The Steady/Stable Parent

Natural Strengths:
Easygoing, patient and a good listener
Natural Limitations:
Unwilling to take charge and indecisive
Pushed to an extreme, the steady parent can become too accommodating.

- High "***S***" parents are very family-oriented and loyal to their children. They like staying home with their kids and always have time for them. They enjoy traditional, customary family events... "Every Christmas we go to Grandma's!"
- They fear loss of security that can come as the result of change. They like stable, routine schedules.
- They speak softly and empathetically. They ask "feeling" questions.
- They seek to maintain a warm, secure home. They need sincere appreciation for all that they do.

High "*S*" parents can keep their strengths from becoming limitations by...
- Taking the initiative when appropriate.
- Learning that change is inevitable and can often present opportunities for growth.
- Speaking up when they are upset about something rather than internalizing their feelings. They need to express their hurts and needs.
- Doing one thing a week that fills their own emotional tank, which they so readily empty for others.

The Cautious/Compliant Parent

Natural Strengths:
Accurate and sets high standards
Natural Limitations:
Too critical, meticulous and strict
Pushed to an extreme, the cautious parent can become too perfectionistic.

- High "**C**" parents like things done "right" or not done at all. The sense of accomplishment of a job well done motivates them to undertake additional tasks.
- They fear being criticized for their work.
- They speak logically and provide a lot of details.
- They seek to maintain high standards and quality. They consistently keep the home in good order.

High "C" parents can keep their strengths from becoming limitations by...

- Accepting the fact that no one is "right" all the time.
- Being careful that cleaning the house, being well-organized and spending the day "according to plan" doesn't get put ahead of taking time to be relational.
- Not being so intense. Unhealthy perfectionism can cause children to feel that their attempts to please a parent will never be good enough.
- Facing up to conflict, rather than avoiding it.
- Verbalizing their feelings more often.

Understanding, Accepting and Affirming Your Child's Style:

The Dominant/Directing Child :

Greatest Felt Needs:
Control and results
Greatest Underlying Need:
To be admired for getting things done

- High "***D***" children are natural-born leaders. As a result, they are extremely strong-willed. They have an overwhelming need to be in control. Needing control is not an option but a driving force in the life of "***D***"children.
- "***D***s" think ahead, plotting for control. They will sense when parents are most vulnerable and then attack. When their parents are preoccupied with something important (for example, talking on the phone), they will take chances that they would not normally take.
- "***D***" children will loudly and angrily declare their disapproval when things don't go their way. Theirs is a logic-based anger, rooted in impatience.
- Because "***D***" children say what they think, they can often hurt people's feelings. They can be blunt, even brutal. If we realize that many times they may not be intentionally trying to hurt someone, we can more easily accept their quick comments and correct them without becoming angry. The effect on others is heightened by their inability to say, "I'm sorry."

Helping "*D*" Children Grow:

- Provide areas where "***D***s" can exercise control while at the same time standing firm when that need for control supersedes parental limits. They need to have definite areas of responsibility and control. The degree of responsibility should increase with the age and development of the child.
- Offer them challenges, competition, change and choices.
- Help each "***D***" child understand that while goals are good, occasional failure is a part of life, and it doesn't mean that he is a failure.
- Teach "***D***s" to accept the importance of limits and boundaries, even if they disagree with them.
- Help them slow down and learn when and how to relax.
- Since "***D***" children deal in reality and results, they are not naturally tuned into the feelings of others. Use their past struggles to help teach them compassion and understanding for others who may be currently experiencing hurt or disappointment.
- When correcting their behavior, focus on actions and be specific as to what needs to be done. Reason with them sensibly and logically. They will tend to rebel when discipline or demands lack a logical explanation or a sense of fairness. In an attempt to control the discipline, they may openly question the way things are done. They will also try to negotiate for reduced punishment. Be brief, to the point and leave. Following any confrontation, give them time to think before approaching them a second time.

The Influencing/Interacting Child

Greatest Felt Needs:
Fun and Excitement
Greatest Underlying Needs:
Enthusiastic approval and constant encouragement

- High "***I***" children are active and need something going on every minute. They are talkative, optimistic and open about their feelings. They are warm and trusting of others. Nobody is a stranger. Everybody in the world is their best friend! They are full of wonderful, creative ideas, but they are often defeated in carrying them out because of their short attention span. They are seldom model students because of their restless nature and happy-go-lucky (undisciplined) approach to life.
- They have difficulty playing alone. They tend to clown around or show-off in order to be the center of attention. Approval and popularity are the overwhelming need for "***I***s". The lack of it can cause a great deal of pain and frustration, for there is no other style that needs social acceptance as badly as this one. Because of this need to impress others, "***I***" children may "go along with the crowd" or be drawn into unwise situations by giving in to peer pressure.
- High "***I***" children are prone to act on impulse and think later.
- When something or someone crosses them, their loving nature can change to immediate anger. Their emotions are a combination of highs and lows. They can quickly go from laughter to tears and back to laughter. Because their moods can change quickly, they can readily adjust to disappointments and make the best of a situation.

- When correcting behavior, look for "*I*s" to create endless excuses. They may also be less than honest. Sometimes they actually believe that their colorful stories are true. Again, this is due to their need to be accepted. Be careful, because your disappointment or anger spells rejection to this style.

Helping "*I*" Children Grow:

- High "*I*" children respond best in a fun, favorable and friendly environment. Constant encouragement is the key. This child will do more through one word of encouragement than he will ever do through criticizing or yelling.
- Start early to teach "*I*" children the discipline of keeping their room clean and the importance of handling money wisely.
- Help them write things down and develop ways to be more organized – including following through with what they start. Understand that you will have to stay right with this child to guarantee any kind of results. Again, they need constant praise to stay at it. However, don't expect miracles; try as they may, high "*I*s" just can't quite make it all click at once.
- Teach them how and when to be more firm and direct in dealing with less than favorable situations.
- In dealing with these children, always consider and affirm their need for social recognition. Know that they always want to do what "everybody" is doing.
- It is especially important to acknowledge what they have accomplished without pointing out how poorly they did it. They function best in a non-judgmental atmosphere.
- This child has a greater need for physical affection than any other style, so parents need to do a lot of hugging, holding, kissing and touching.

The Steady/Stable Child

Greatest Felt Needs:
Peace and Stability
Greatest Underlying Needs:
To be appreciated and valued as a person

- High "***S***" children are the most enjoyable to raise, because they are naturally quiet, easygoing, agreeable and undemanding. They are more comfortable as a listener and participant in a group rather than a talker or leader.
- They like doing the same things in a routine manner. This provides them with a sense of security and stability which is extremely important. They dislike sudden changes.
- They are not usually openly rebellious but may offer considerable resistance. They may smile and agree to do whatever you ask while inside they know they have no desire to comply with your request. They may lie or distort the facts somewhat to avoid any form of conflict. They do not set out to be dishonest, but they may take the chance to avoid conflict.
- They may appear to be stingy or selfish because they are possessive of their belongings.
- While "***S***" children are good listeners and peacemakers, their indecisiveness and lack of initiative can paralyze them with procrastination and inactivity. More active style parents cannot understand why these children seem to have so little ambition.
- Do not expect them to get excited or enthusiastic about things. Accept the fact that they will not jump for joy over new ideas.
- High "***S***" children rarely show a visible expression of anger. They are the most underdeveloped

personality in the area of anger because of their fear of conflict and confrontation. They actually lose all thought processes and go mentally blank. Unlike the "***D***" child who responds to hurt or disappointment with anger, the "***S***" child responds to situations that call for anger with hurt or sadness.

- You may need a heavy hand with a "***D***" and sometimes an "***I***", but the same strong language will depress a "***C***" and overwhelm an "***S***".

Helping "S" Children Grow:

- High "***S***" children respond best in an environment where there is stability, security and few quick changes. If change is necessary, discuss how the change will affect them and give them time to adjust.
- Provide personal assurances, support and sincere appreciation. They have a great desire to please others. Be patient with them. Remember that they have an overwhelming fear of confrontation and conflict. They also have a deep need to feel special to someone, so don't ignore them just because they are not demanding.
- Teach them to be more assertive with people when appropriate.
- Encourage them to do things differently.
- Encourage them to express their feelings more often, especially feelings of anger. Help them find a creative outlet for repressed anger through "talking out" their responses to conflict in a safe, nonthreatening environment.
- Help them set goals and reward them for achieving their goals. They will work better if they earn a gold star or have a chart of duties to check off.
- Teach them how to make decisions on their own by starting early to present choices to them.

The Cautious/Compliant Child

Greatest Felt Needs:
Perfection and sensitivity
Greatest Underlying Need:
Continual reassurance (a desire for you to sense and respond to their needs and feelings without them being verbalized)

- High "**C**" children are intent on doing the "right" thing. They strive to avoid mistakes that may cause them to appear not to meet their own high standards. These children feel that they can be most correct when doing things by themselves.
- These children become upset when their standards are violated by someone who should "know better." Under pressure (when things are not "right"), they become visibly anxious and worried.
- They ask questions that will tell them how, when, where and, especially, why, something should be done. Be prepared to answer their questions in a patient manner.
- High "**C**" children tend to do their work neatly. They like things in their proper place and are bothered by wrong answers or red check marks on their papers. They are shy about speaking before the whole class. They are sensitive children and don't like to take chances that might make them look foolish. They observe, ask and seek information. They make some surprisingly logical connections for their ages. They have great potential to be excellent students because of their tendency toward high standards.
- High "**C**" children desire personal attention and continual reassurance. However, while they want

appreciation and recognition of their accomplishments, they also may be suspicious of compliments. Knowing this should help parents give sincere, loving compliments, and not be upset if the response is, "What did you really mean by that?"

- Accept the fact that they like peace and quiet. They need time alone. Like the "**S**" child, they do not like surprises or things to change quickly.
- High "**C**" children seldom respond to any person or situation with immediate anger. When someone hurts or offends "**C**s", they simply tuck the hurt away inside them. When another offense comes, it too may be stored. At the same time, they may begin planning alternative strategies to avoid being hurt in the future or to get back at the offender.
- When correcting behavior, focus on the facts and why what they did was unacceptable. Remember, they can be very sensitive to criticism. Do not berate them or put them down. Give them the opportunity to ask questions. After discipline, go back and reassure them of your love and support. Help them talk about what they are feeling.

Helping "C" Children Grow:

- High "**C**" children feel that if you really loved them, you would be sensitive to their needs, even without them telling you their needs. Therefore, you must draw them out with "what-are-you-thinking/feeling" kinds of questions in order to help them verbalize what's going on inside. Help these children find words to express what they are feeling.
- Allow them time to do quality work. Don't rush them. When they procrastinate, it's because they want to do the job "right."

- Never tell them that their problems or concerns are stupid. Never tell them that they should not be so picky. If you do, you communicate that their approach to life is not valued and that only reinforces their feelings of inferiority.
- Help them to develop a greater tolerance for conflict and imperfection. No one is right all of the time – not even them.
- Recognize that they have a tendency to have a critical spirit and to complain. Begin early to help them reduce this tendency.
- Because their personal standards are so high, they often do not meet them. Therefore, high "**C**" children constantly struggle with feelings of inferiority and inadequacy. Work on building their self-esteem by focusing on who they are, not just what they do. Be persistent in reassuring and affirming a "**C**" about his high value as a person. Be specific as to how his natural strengths and abilities can produce great results in the future.

Understanding the High "*D*" Child

Insight #1 – Personality Style

Things you will notice as they grow and mature...

Style: Dominant – Determined

Style Description:

Dominant/Directing, determined, decisive, active, strong-willed, self-confident, quick with decisions and answers, takes risks, competitive, persistent, fast-paced and task-oriented

Main Features – This child...

- has a strong ego
- dares to be different
- is not afraid to take risks
- likes to be in control
- is goal-oriented
- likes new and varied activities
- is a self-starter

Value to Group – This child...

- is results-oriented
- is motivated to get results
- is good at organizing events
- likes to be competitive
- speaks out openly
- has adventure and "go" in his blood

Danger Zone – At times, this child...

- may appear argumentative
- oversteps authority
- can be "pushy" or impatient
- may act belligerently
- does not like routine

Basic Goal or Motivation –

- Motivated by being a leader and taking charge, being in control
- Wants immediate results, choices, challenges and tangible rewards

Blocked goals become…Fears…

- Fears losing control and being taken advantage of by others

Insight #2 – Attitudes and Preferences

The "*D*" Type Child Might Say…

"I like to think about the future."
"I like new ideas."
"I like a challenge."
"I like activities that change a lot."
"I like to make things happen."
"I like to show I can do it myself."
"I like things to move fast."
"I like to be respected for what I can do."
"I don't like being told what to do."
"I don't like having to think about little things."

Emotions and Behavior Under Pressure…

Impatient, demanding, defiant, blunt, bossy, bragging, quick-tempered, inflexible, keeps fighting for what they want, comes on too strong, insensitive to the needs of others.

Insight #3 – Motivational Tips

Each Personality Style Has Different "Hot Buttons."

They Might Say…

"I like to be in charge."
"I like it when things change fast."
"When I work, I work hard."

"When I play, I play hard."
"I like to have power."
"I'll try something if I think it will work."
"I like to make decisions."
"I like new jobs to do."
"I like to be respected for what I can do."
"I like to be the boss."
"I don't like always doing the same old things all the time."
"I don't like doing slow or boring jobs."

If "*D*" Children are Underachieving… Important Questions to Consider…

Are they being challenged?
Do they have opportunities to be in control of something?
Do they have some "say so" in the situation?

Insight #4 – Ideal Environment

Each Style has a "Comfort Zone"…

I Like An Environment Where…

I can be in charge of myself and others.
There are a lot of things to do and do well.
I can decide what is important and when to do it.
I can tell that I am getting better and better.
What I do is important.
People will notice how well I do and let me do more.
I can look good.

Growth Areas – Teach Them To…

- accept the importance of limits and boundaries.
- deal with their anger in constructive ways.
- be more patient when things don't happen on their timetable.
- be more sensitive to the feelings of others.

Insight #5 – Communication Tips

When talking with this Personality Type, it is best to…

Get to the point.
Tell me what you want…quickly!
Tell me **WHAT** you want me to do.
Show me how this will solve my problem.
Don't get too emotional.
Give me the facts, not your opinion.
Show me how I can be a winner.
Prove that I can respect what you say.

Correcting Inappropriate Behavior

- Focus on actions and be specific as to **WHAT** needs to be done.
- Get right to the point.
- Be firm.
- Refuse to argue.
- Calmly give logical reasons.
- Following discipline, give them time to think.
- They will tend to rebel if discipline lacks a logical explanation or a sense of fairness.

Insight #6 – Twenty Encouraging Words

Praise That Reflects Your Child's Strengths

Say to your "***D***" Child…

"I like that you are a determined person."
"I like that you have confidence in yourself."
"I like that you aren't easily sidetracked."
"I like that you can't be pushed into doing something that you don't want to do."
"I like that you say exactly what you think."
"I like that you set your mind on something and go after it with everything you have."

"I like that you feel able to handle things on your own."
"I like that you really stick with things that interest you."
"I like that you are committed and decisive."
"I like that you are assertive."
"I like that you are independent and capable."
"I like that you charge into new situations without fear."
"I like that you are quick to respond to a situation, and that you seek solutions."
"I like that you know what you want and go after it."
"I like that you really play hard to win."
"I like that you have a very honest way of expressing exactly what you think about things."
"I like that you like to get results when you do things."
"I like that you have a lot of drive."
"I like that you have a strong will."
"I like that you are up-front with people."

Insight #7 – A Word of Encouragement About Your Child

Explaining Strengths and Weaknesses

If you parent "***D***" type children, you may think they argue or "fight" with you too much. But remember, they have a ton of nervous energy and are just trying to find the right direction in which to channel it! Their greatest fear is that someone will take advantage of them. They need to be allowed to make choices and to have some input and control in their "rules" and boundaries. They love to be in charge, and they like a personal challenge. Teaching them to accept limits, even when they disagree, is important. They need to develop more patience and be willing to help others more. Their anger will always hinder them unless it is used constructively. They need to remember that *failure is an event, not a person.*

> **Secret Tip:** *"Before you can be **in** authority, you must first learn to be **under** authority."*

Understanding the High "*I*" Child

Insight #1 – Personality Style

Things you will notice as they grow and mature...

Style: Inspirational – Influencing

Style Description:

Interactive/Influencing, enthusiastic, entertaining, persuasive, imaginative, inspirational, optimistic, "life-of-the-party," energetic, self-promoting, talkative, fast-paced and people-oriented

Main Features – This child...

- is outgoing and talkative
- likes to express ideas or stories
- is impulsive
- is usually optimistic
- likes to entertain others
- is persuasive and persistent
- loves recognition and rewards

Value to Group – This child...

- likes to make people happy
- makes new friends easily
- has a good sense of humor
- is warm, friendly and trusting
- is transparent with his feelings
- is creative in solving problems
- likes to make people laugh

Danger Zone – At times, this child...

- tends to be disorganized
- is inattentive to detail
- speaks before thinking
- lacks follow-through skills

- prefers talking over working
- is overly optimistic, sometimes unrealistic

Basic Goal or Motivation –

- Motivated by involvement with others
- Public praise and social recognition
- Wants attention, approval and popularity

Blocked goals become...Fears...

- Fears rejection and loss of approval

Insight #2 – Attitudes and Preferences

The "*I*" Type Child Might Say...

"I like to talk about what I think and feel."
"I like to be part of a group of people."
"I like it when nobody argues."
"I like it when everybody is friendly."
"I like lots of parties and fun things to do."
"I like surprises."
"I don't like details."
"I don't like bossy people who give orders."
"I don't like to fight with anybody."

Emotions and Behavior Under Pressure...

Careless, impulsive, disorganized, unrealistic, overly sentimental, overdraws their emotional bank account, may blow up and verbally attack

Insight #3 – Motivational Tips

Each Personality Style Has Different "Hot Buttons."

They Might Say...

"I like a lot of friends."
"I like it when other people like me."
"I like it when other people handle the small stuff."
"I like it when people are happy and smiling and laughing."

"I like it when people say that I am doing a good job."
"I like quick jobs."
"I want everybody to like me."
"I don't like it when people tell me what to do."
"I like to go and do lots of things."
"I like it when people tell others that I am important."
"I forget to do things."

If "*I*" Children are Underachieving... Important Questions to Consider...

Do they need more flexibility?
Do they need more visible recognition, praise or rewards? (They like public attention, affection, stickers or ribbons that acknowledge a "good job.")

Insight #4 – Ideal Environment

Each Style has a "Comfort Zone"...

I Like An Environment Where...

There are people to talk to.
I am praised for my good work.
I can get other people to do what I want.
Everyone has a good attitude.
People accept me and are not snobby.
People I work with like me and are happy most of the time.
I don't have to check little things or do them over and over.

Growth Areas – Teach Them...

- discipline, orderliness and the importance of money.
- to write things down and develop ways to be more organized. Don't expect too much, however!
- to be firm and direct.
- that not going along with the crowd can be beneficial.

Insight #5 – Communication Tips

When talking with this Personality Type, it is best to...

Keep things friendly.
Let me say what I am thinking about.
Tell me **WHO** else is doing what you want me to do.
Help me to do what I say I am going to do.
Tell me about what others have done.
Don't forget time to talk or play with my friends.
Give me quick jobs with rewards.
Show me that you want to be my friend, too.
Notice the good things that I do.

Correcting Inappropriate Behavior

- Provide details of how things must change, and then develop a plan.
- Expect them to create excuses.
- Remember that your anger or disapproval spells rejection for this child.
- They may also be less than honest, because they do not want to lose your approval.

Insight #6 – Twenty Encouraging Words

Praise That Reflects Your Child's Strengths

Say to your "*I*" Child...

"I like that you are an outgoing person."
"I like that you have lots of enthusiasm – it's contagious."
"I like that you have a wonderful sense of humor."
"I like that you are eager to participate in everything that is going on."
"I like that you have such a creative imagination."
"I like that you are really flexible."
"I like that you are full of surprises."
"I like that you are full of energy."
"I like that you really like people and want them to like you."

"I like that you really enjoy being with people."
"I like that you make others feel comfortable."
"I like that you seem to look for the best in people and situations."
"I like that you don't seem bothered by loose ends and details."
"I like that you have a happy spirit about you."
"I like that you are fun to be with."
"I like that you share your thoughts and feelings easily."
"I like that you have a special ability to motivate people."
"I like that you are a great storyteller."
"I like that you are so gifted at expressing yourself."
"I like that you recharge your batteries around people."

Insight #7 – A Word of Encouragement About Your Child

Explaining Strengths and Weaknesses

If you parent "***I***" type children, you may be tired – they have a lot of energy! They love to be on the go. They have lots of friends, and they usually want visitors and playmates over to the house. Their greatest fear is rejection or loss of social approval from their friends. They need help in learning how to become organized. You cannot simply say, "Get organized!" It is something you must show them. They have trouble staying focused and on track. It is difficult for them to manage their time – it gets away quickly! They need to learn that their emotions may get them into trouble. They want to be liked so much, that they may try to impress others and end up in trouble. They must know when to walk away from trouble.

Secret Tip: *"It's nice to be important, but it's **more important** to be nice."*

Understanding the High "*S*" Child

Insight #1 – Personality Style

Things you will notice as they grow and mature...

Style: Supportive – Steady

Style Description:

Steady/Stable, sensitive, sincere, sticks with tasks, easygoing, cooperative, patient, possessive, good listener, slow-paced and people-oriented

Main Features – This child...

- is easygoing and mild-mannered
- does not like confrontation
- likes a stable environment
- needs appreciation and security
- is warm and friendly
- is understanding and patient
- avoids conflict or strife

Value to Group – This child...

- is a team player
- gets along well with others
- has good follow-through skills
- is loyal and dependable
- likes to know what is expected
- works well under authority
- is a good listener

Danger Zone – At times, this child...

- has difficulty establishing priorities
- is sometimes overly sensitive
- tends to be indecisive
- "stuffs" too much inside

- avoids or resists change
- is a people pleaser

Basic Goal or Motivation –

- Motivated by helping others
- Motivated by sincere appreciation
- Wants to keep things the same – structured and peaceful

Blocked goals become…Fears…

- Fears sudden, unplanned change and loss of stability

Insight #2 – Attitudes and Preferences

The "*S*" Type Child Might Say…

"I like it when people work together and get along."
"I like to do the same things most of the time."
"I like to work on one thing at a time."
"I like sticking with what works."
"I like things to stay the same."
"I like knowing what will happen next."
"I like ideas that work and are easy to do."
"I don't like angry people."
"I don't like it when things change quickly."
"I don't like arguing or tough talk."

Emotions and Behavior Under Pressure…

Indecisive, slows things down to avoid change, becomes even more quiet, gives in, but may be internally rebelling, extremely possessive and sensitive

Insight #3 – Motivational Tips

Each Personality Style Has Different "Hot Buttons."

They Might Say…

"I like it when things stay the same."
"I like to please people."
"I like to be around happy people."

"I like to see people be happy."
"I like doing the same things."
"I like knowing what will happen next."
"I like it when people appreciate me."
"I like to finish my work."
"I don't like starting new jobs."
"I don't like to work with people who are too pushy."
"I don't like dangerous things."
"I don't mind being told what to do."

If "*S*" Children are Underachieving... Important Questions to Consider...

Do they understand how to do the job?
Is the task broken down into clear, specific steps?
Do they feel appreciated?"

Insight #4 – Ideal Environment

Each Style has a "Comfort Zone"...

I Like An Environment Where...

I feel like I belong with everybody.
I know people really appreciate me.
Things pretty much stay the same every day.
No one makes me do things quickly.
I can count on things staying the same.
We do a few things, and we do them very well.
I know what is safe for me to do and to try.

Growth Areas – Teach Them ...

- to be more assertive, decisive, flexible and accepting of change.
- to look for new ways to do things.
- to take more initiative.
- to be less possessive.
- to not hold grudges.
- to learn to say, "No."

Insight #5 – Communication Tips

When talking with this Personality Type, it is best to...

Show that you care about me.
Tell me **HOW** you want me to do it.
Be patient with me.
Explain things calmly and clearly.
Give me time to think about changes before they happen.
Tell me why what you want me to do is important.
Be there to help me through changes.
Tell me why I should do what you want me to do.
Don't act scary or angry.

Correcting Inappropriate Behavior

- Focus on **HOW** things need to be different.
- Draw out how they are feeling.
- Remember that they are very sensitive and fear confrontation.
- They are not generally openly rebellious, but they can be stubbornly resistant.

Insight #6 – Twenty Encouraging Words

Praise That Reflects Your Child's Strengths

Say to your "*S*" Child...

"I like that you are a caring person."
"I like that you are an accepting person."
"I like that you can feel other people's hurts and stresses."
"I like that you like to check things out before you jump in."
"I like that you want to know what to expect."
"I like that you change, even though it is difficult for you."
"I like that you are easy to talk to."
"I like that you do things step-by-step."
"I like that you don't rush into decisions."

"I like that you go out of your way to get along with people."
"I like that you are a good listener."
"I like that you are compassionate and tenderhearted."
"I like that you always follow through."
"I like that you don't look for conflict or try to make waves."
"I like that you seem to be so easygoing."
"I like that you have a calming influence on other people."
"I like that you don't seem pressured by time."
"I like that you are a trusting type of person."
"I like that you give people the benefit of the doubt."
"I like that you need time to yourself to recharge."

Insight #7 – A Word of Encouragement About Your Child

Explaining Strengths and Weaknesses

If you parent "***S***" type children, you need to remember that each one is special. All children are special – however, the "***S***" types are the ones who get "lost in the shuffle." They require a little extra care because of their emotional sensitivity. Their greatest fear is loss of security or stability. They need the added touch of quantity time, not just quality time. You can help them most by allowing them to express how they feel. As they grow up, you will need to teach and remind them to discern objectively the actions and intentions of others. You will have to encourage them to take initiative and be more decisive. Help them to learn to be less possessive and not hold grudges.

Secret Tip: *"Don't be afraid to say, 'What part of NO don't you understand?'"*

Understanding the High "**C**" Child

Insight #1 – Personality Style

Things you will notice as they grow and mature…
Style: Cautious – Correct

Style Description:
Cautious/Conscientious, correct, logical, analytical, high standards, perfectionist, precise, reserved, contemplative, courteous, slow-paced and task-oriented

Main Features – This child…

- likes to be precise
- does not like confusion
- thinks things through
- demonstrates caution and curiosity
- wants things to make sense
- prefers to be quiet and careful
- enjoys learning the facts

Value to Group – This child…

- is a good organizer
- knows how to follow directions
- wants things done correctly
- is even-tempered
- can understand a situation well
- has high personal standards
- likes to be thorough

Danger Zone – At times, this child…

- finds fault too easily
- can be too critical
- becomes anxious and nervous
- worries about "what if" too much

- may withdraw "into his shell"
- sometimes misses the big picture

Basic Goal or Motivation –

- Motivated by achieving their own high standards
- Wants to be correct and to avoid mistakes at all costs

Blocked goals become...Fears...

- Fears personal criticism of their work and making mistakes

Insight #2 – Attitudes and Preferences

The "C" Type Child Might Say...

"I like practical ideas and suggestions."
"I like to know exactly what you want me to do."
"I like to finish what I start."
"I like to do the same thing most of the time."
"I like doing things I know I am good at."
"I like clear directions so that I don't make mistakes."
"I like things I have to think about and plan."
"I worry about things a lot."
"I don't like messy places."
"I don't like arguing or fighting."

Emotions and Behavior Under Pressure...
Strict and judgmental as well as overly perfectionistic and sensitive, becomes anxious, worried, depressed, melancholy, and gets bogged down in the "paralysis of analysis," tends to withdraw in order to plan the next move

Insight #3 – Motivational Tips

Each Personality Style Has Different "Hot Buttons."

They Might Say...
"I like quality."
"I like small important things."

"I like things that make sense."
"I like plans and diagrams."
"I like to solve problems using my brain."
"I like to know I am doing well."
"I like to be organized."
"I like to be told when I do good work."
"I like doing things step-by-step."
"I expect myself and others to do a good job."
"I want to do everything right."
"I don't like silly people."

If "C" Children are Underachieving... Important Questions to Consider...

Do they have enough time to do quality work?
Do they understand **WHY** something needs to be done?
Have you provided them with enough information and details?

Insight #4 – Ideal Environment

Each Style has a "Comfort Zone"...

I Like An Environment Where...

People know what they are doing.
I don't have people checking up on me all the time.
I am not rushing to get the job done.
Everybody knows what they are responsible to do.
I know exactly what people want from me.
Changes happen slowly and with careful planning.
I am rewarded for finding ways to do things better.

Growth Areas – Teach Them ...

- to develop a greater tolerance for conflict and human imperfections.
- to verbalize their feelings.
- to take more risks.

- to get involved with others who have complementary strengths.
- to listen empathetically.

Insight #5 – Communication Tips

When talking with this Personality Type, it is best to…

Show me the good and bad behind the plan.
Make sure we understand exactly what we agree on.
Tell me **WHY** you want me to do it.
Give me facts that I can trust.
Show me how I fit in.
Have good answers ready for my questions.
Be patient and take your time in giving me details.
Be clear in what you think and what you want.
Make sure that there are no surprises.

Correcting Inappropriate Behavior

- Focus on the facts and **WHY** what they did was unacceptable.
- Give them the opportunity to ask questions.
- Be prepared to give detailed explanations.
- Be sure to reassure them of your love and support.
- Remember that they are sensitive to criticism.
- Do not put them down or berate them.

Insight #6 – Twenty Encouraging Words

Praise That Reflects Your Child's Strengths

Say to your "C" Child…

"I like that you tend to be a quiet person."
"I like that you have such high standards."
"I like that you always try to do your best work."
"I like that you listen to what others say and feel."
"I like that you like things to be organized."
"I like that you do things precisely and accurately."

"I like that you want to understand all you can about what you are planning."
"I like that you like to do things in a logical way."
"I like that you seem to weigh things out carefully."
"I like that you are a good evaluator."
"I like that you like to think about things and then decide."
"I like that you are a serious person."
"I like that you think deeply about things."
"I like that you like things to be 'just right.'"
"I like that you have a questioning mind."
"I like that you are interested in key details."
"I like that you enjoy spending time by yourself."
"I like that you are a trustworthy person."
"I like that you find quiet time to think and grow inside."
"I like that you are a good example for others."

Insight #7 – A Word of Encouragement About Your Child

Explaining Strengths and Weaknesses

If you parent "**C**" type children, you may wonder if "**C**s" ever run out of questions. "**C**s" have a curious nature about them. They desire to learn what makes things "tick." Their greatest fear is personal criticism – having someone attack or make fun of their work or effort. It will be helpful if you teach them that all people are in various stages of growth. They need to develop a greater tolerance for the mistakes of others. They need to be allowed to verbalize their thoughts and ask questions without feeling "put down." (Make sure your "**C**" child knows his high value as a person.) Explain as many "**WHY**s" as you can. Reassure and affirm their quality work. Show them patience and kindness; it will pay good rewards.

> **Secret Tip:** *"People don't **care** how much you know until they **know** how much you care."*

101 Ways to Praise a Student or a Child...

1. Wow!
2. Way to go!
3. Super!
4. You're special!
5. Outstanding!
6. Excellent!
7. Great!
8. Good!
9. Neat!
10. Well Done!
11. Remarkable!
12. I knew you could do it!
13. I'm proud of you!
14. Fantastic!
15. Super Star!
16. Nice Work!
17. Looking Good!
18. You're all over this!
19. Beautiful!
20. Now You're Flying!
21. You're catching on.
22. Now you've got it.

23. You're incredible.
24. Bravo!
25. You're fantastic!
26. Hurray for you!
27. You're on target!
28. You're on your way!
29. How nice!
30. How smart!
31. Good job!
32. That's incredible!
33. Hot Dog!
34. Dynamite!
35. You're beautiful!
36. You're unique.
37. Nothing can stop you now!
38. Good for you.
39. I like you.
40. You're a winner!
41. Remarkable job.
42. Beautiful work!
43. Spectacular!
44. You're spectacular!
45. You are so funny!
46. You're precious.
47. Great discovery!
48. You've discovered the secret!
49. You figured it out!
50. Fantastic job!

51. Hip, hip, hurray!
52. Bingo!
53. Magnificent!
54. Marvelous!
55. Terrific!
56. You're important.
57. Phenomenal!
58. You're sensational!
59. Super work!
60. Creative job.
61. Super job!
62. You really get results!
63. Exceptional performance.
64. You're a real trooper!
65. You are responsible.
66. You are exciting!
67. I am so impressed!
68. What an imagination!
69. What a good listener!
70. You are fun.
71. You're growing up.
72. You tried hard.
73. You care.
74. Beautiful sharing.
75. Outstanding performance.
76. You're a good friend.
77. I trust you.
78. You're important.

79. You mean a lot to me.
80. You make me feel happy.
81. You are an important part of the team.
82. You've got a friend.
83. You make me laugh.
84. You brighten my day.
85. I respect you.
86. You mean the world to me.
87. That's correct.
88. You're a joy.
89. You're a treasure.
90. You're wonderful.
91. You're perfect.
92. Awesome!
93. Now you're talking!
94. You are A-Okay!
95. You made my day!
96. That's the best!
97. A big hug!
98. A big kiss!
99. Tremendous!
100. Hey…I love it!
101. A+ Job!

… and when you say any of these words - remember to smile - because your smile is worth an extra 1000 words!

To learn more about personality styles
and to get four free online lessons,
please go to:
www.personalityinsights.com
On the home page click on the free
offer icon that says:
"Take the 4-part online course for
better relationships."
We hope you enjoy the lessons!